This book belongs to: _____

Teacher: _____

Grade: _____

The
Catholic
Bible Story
Workbook

www.firesidebibles.com

The Catholic Bible Story Workbook

IMPRIMATUR: Most Rev. Thomas J. Olmsted, J.C.D.
Coadjutor Bishop of Wichita
January 1, 2000

NIHIL OBSTAT: Rev. John P. Lanzrath, S.T.L.
Censor

Published by
Fireside Bible Publishers
Wichita, Kansas
© 2000

Printed in the United States of America

The Catholic Bible Story Workbook

Old Testament

New Testament

A Timeline of a Journey of Faith

The Creation of the World – God's Gift of Man and the Universe
Noah and the Ark – A New Beginning
Tower of Babel – The Folly of Mankind

1850 B.C. Abraham – Our Father in Faith

1800 B.C. Jacob and Esau – Christ's Lineage Restored

1775 B.C. Jacob - A Patriarch of Israel

1725 B.C. Joseph – The Journey Into Egypt

1300 B.C. Moses – God's Messenger of Freedom

1250 B.C. Plagues on Egypt – God's Passover Blessing

1250 B.C. Red Sea – God's Promise Fulfilled

1220 B.C. Ten Commandments – God Speaks to His People

1210 B.C. Manna in the Desert – God Sustains His People

1200 B.C. Battle of Jericho – The Return to The Promised Land

1150 B.C. Samson – God's Judgement through Strength

1100 B.C. Ruth and Naomi – Loyalty and Love Defined

1015 B.C. David and Goliath – Faith's Triumph over Evil

1000 B.C. David the King of Israel – The Golden Age of Israel

960 B.C. Solomon – God's Blessing of Wisdom

750 B.C. Jonah – A Lesson in Forgiveness

550 B.C. Daniel in the Lions' Den – Trusting in God

1 A.D. Annunciation and Birth of Jesus – God's Salvation Foretold

1 A.D. Presentation of Jesus in the Temple – The Messiah Recognized

12 A.D. Finding in the Temple – God's Presence Revealed

30 A.D. John the Baptist – A Call to Prepare

31 A.D. Twelve Apostles – God's Chosen Few

31 A.D. Wedding at Cana – A Miraculous Lesson

32 A.D. Sermon on the Mount – God's Laws Simplified

33 A.D. Raising of Lazarus – God's Power over Death

33 A.D. Last Supper – God's Gift to the Centuries

33 A.D. Crucifixion and Resurrection – The Prophecies Fulfilled

33 A.D. Road to Emmaus – God in Our Midst

The Story of Creation
Genesis 1:1-31; 2:1-7,18-25

The Bible tells us that in the **beginning** there were no plants or animals, no rivers or seas, no mountains or valleys and no sun during the day or moon at night. There were no boys or girls, no sisters or brothers, no parents or grandparents or friends or people of any kind. There was only **God**. Therefore, to show His love for us, God created the world and all things in it. The heavens and the earth and all things in them appeared instantly as God created them - step by step.

When God began His **creation**, the world was a dark and dreary place. A mighty wind blew over the waters that covered the earth. Then God said "Let there be light," and at that very moment a brilliant light, even brighter than the sun, was present everywhere. God separated that light which He called **day** from the darkness, which He called **night**. This was the end of the first day.

On the second day, God made a great dome to separate the waters above it from the waters below. He called this dome the **sky**.

On the third day God gathered all the water on the earth into one place He called the sea, the dry land that was left He called the earth. Then on His command, the earth brought forth every kind of plant and tree that soon covered the earth. This was the end of the third day. God saw how beautiful and how good all of these things were at the end of each day.

On the fourth day God created the sun to light the day

and the moon and stars to light the night. God put in place that day how the sun and moon help us keep track of the passing of not only the days but also the years in time. This was the end of the fourth day.

On the fifth day, God **commanded** the waters of the sea to be full of fish, both great and small, and ordered that the air be filled with birds of every kind. God commanded the animals to be fruitful and multiply. This was the end of the fifth day.

On the sixth day, God created all the animals and creeping things that covered the earth. The land was filled with living **creatures** that roamed in the forests, grazed upon the plains, and moved about everywhere. Then God said: "Let us make man in our image, after our **likeness**." God created the first man named **Adam** and later the first woman named **Eve** to share in the beauty of His newly created world.

Adam and Eve were more special than all previous creations. They were created in the likeness of God and were the completion of His creative work. Because they were created in His likeness, God gave Adam and Eve command of the fish of the sea, the birds of the air, the cattle, and all the wild animals of the earth and every creeping thing upon the earth. God looked at everything He had created and found that it was good. This was the end of the sixth day.

On the seventh day God rested from all the work He had done. He blessed the seventh day and made it holy.

Adam and Eve were placed in the **Garden of Eden,** the most beautiful spot on God's newly created world, and given authority over all its creatures. God commanded them to "multiply and to replenish the earth," and to glorify God and carry out His Divine will.

Name: _____   Date: _____

Key Words - The Story of Creation

Adam	creation	Eve	likeness
beginning	creatures	Garden of Eden	night
commanded	day	God	sky

A. Best Match

Circle <u>all</u> the terms that fit with each day of creation.

Day 1	Night	Water	Day	Moon
Day 2	Birds	Sky	Stars	Trees
Day 3	Seas	Trees	Man	Stars
Day 4	Moon	Flowers	Stars	Sun
Day 5	Fish	Moon	Birds	Man
Day 6	Man	Cows	Seas	Fish
Day 7	Horses	Flowers	Eve	Rest

B. Fill in the Blanks

Unscramble the letters to fill in the missing **key words**.

1. God _____ the seas to be full of fish on the fifth day.
   (ddaomcmne)

2. Living _____ roamed the whole earth.
   (tseeacrur)

3. Before God started His _____the world was dark and dreary.
   (tcrinoea)

4. God made man in His own _____.
   (nsesklie)

5. In the _____ there was only God.
   (nninggbei)

C. Matching

Match the **key words** on the left with the correct phrase or word on the right.

____ 1. Creation	A. the first man
____ 2. Day	B. the first woman
____ 3. Commanded	C. at the start
____ 4. Creatures	D. ordered
____ 5. Likeness	E. something that is made
____ 6. Adam	F. darkness
____ 7. Eve	G. light
____ 8. God	H. dome of waters above
____ 9. Garden of Eden	I. living beings
____ 10. Beginning	J. Adam & Eve lived there
____ 11. Night	K. in the beginning there was only
____ 12. Sky	L. image

D. Essay Questions

What was God's most special creation and why was it so special?

_____

_____

_____

_____

It is said that the Garden of Eden was the most beautiful spot on earth. Where do you think the most beautiful spot on earth is today?

_____

_____

_____

The Story of Noah and the Ark
Genesis 6, 7, 8, 9

There was a day when God looked down on the earth and saw only one good man. His name was **Noah**, a Sethite and a descendent of Enoch. Noah, unlike all the other people of that day, found **favor** with God because he was a good and upright man. He was the only person who did what was right.

Everywhere around Noah, the world was full of evil and wickedness. All the people had turned away from God. They thought only about themselves and their sinful ways. God was so disappointed at seeing how evil man had become, He was sorry that He had ever created him. Therefore, in His grief, God decided to wipe out from the earth all the people He had created. In fact, He even included the destruction of all other living things. But God saved Noah.

To rid the world of evil, God planned a **flood** to cover the whole earth- even the mountains! The only people God saved were Noah, his wife and his three sons Shem, Ham, and Japeth and their wives. God instructed Noah to build a big boat He called an **ark**. God gave Noah exact instructions on how to build the ark and Noah obeyed. It was to be made out of gopherwood. It was 300 cubits long, 50 **cubits** wide and 30 cubits tall. A cubit is about 18 inches. The ark was over 3 stories tall and longer than a football field. It had an open-

ing at the top for day-light to let the light and air enter. The ark also had a window or hatch that could be opened and closed.

When the ark was completed, God told Noah to take his wife and sons and their wives into the ark. He was also instructed to bring two of every **species** of animal in the world with all their food and sup-plies on board. Then God shut the door and the rains began to pour down upon the earth. It rained for forty days and forty nights without stopping.

The waters rose higher and higher until at last even the tallest mountain peak was under water – completely covered by the flood – just as God had said. All creatures on earth **perished** in the flood. All this time, Noah and his family and all the animals were safe in the ark floating above the destruction.

After one hundred and fifty days, God made a wind sweep over the earth. The water began to recede and finally the ark came to rest on **Mount Ararat**. After the mountaintops appeared Noah waited forty days to send out a raven to see if it was safe to go out but the bird did not return. Seven days later, he sent out a **dove** but since it could find no place to land, it came back and landed on his hand. Noah waited seven more days and then sent the dove out again. This time it returned with an **olive twig** in its beak so Noah knew that the water had gone down enough that trees were growing. He waited another seven days and sent the dove out once more, but this time it did not return to him so he was sure the earth was dry again.

Then God said to Noah "Go out of the ark, together with your wife and sons and your sons' wives. Bring out with you every living thing,... and let them

abound on the earth, breeding and multiplying on it." So Noah, his family, and all the animals came out of the ark. Noah immediately built an altar and gave thanks to the Lord for His love in saving them. God blessed Noah and his family and made a **covenant** (promise) with them never to destroy the earth by flood again. As a sign of this covenant, God told them that every time a **rainbow** appears in the sky it would serve as a reminder of the promise He made to all mortal creatures.

Noah lived three hundred and fifty years after the flood. He died at the age of nine hundred and fifty. Noah was spared by God because he obeyed God's laws in every way. Because of his love for God, Noah was blessed with descendants who became the fathers and mothers of all people who were to follow.

Name: _____ Date: _____

Key Words - The Story of Noah and the Ark

ark	dove	Mount Ararat	perished
covenant	favor	Noah	rainbow
cubits	flood	olive twig	species

A. A rainbow of words

Fill in the answers from left to right to complete the rainbow of **key words**.

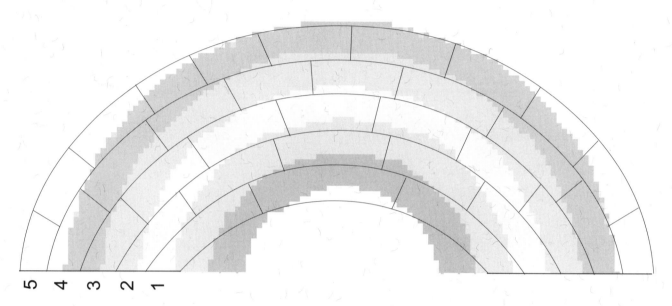

5   4   3   2   1

1. Noah's boat
2. It destroyed the earth.
3. Noah took two of each _____ of animals.
4. a promise
5. where the ark landed

B. Matching

Match the **key word** on the left with the correct word or phrase on the right.

_____ 1. Species   A. each of these is equal to 18 inches

_____ 2. Perished   B. died

_____ 3. Covenant   C. approved of or liked

_____ 4. Favor   D. a promise

_____ 5. Cubits   E. a group of related living things

C. Fill in the Blanks

Fill in the blanks with the correct **key words**. Use the coded letters to reveal the mystery answers.

1. When the ___ ___ ___ ___ that ___ ___ ___ ___ sent out came back with
                  12   14

   an ___ ___ ___ ___ ___   ___ ___ ___ ___ he knew the water was going
         4   1   8

   down enough for the trees to grow.

2. When God caused it to rain everything and everyone on earth
   ___ ___ ___ ___ ___ ___ ___ except those on the ___ ___ ___ .
       15   9 16   7   11

3. Noah was saved from the ___ ___ ___ ___ ___ since he found
                                     13

   ___ ___ ___ ___ ___ with God.
     5

4. God reminds everyone of his ___ ___ ___ ___ ___ ___ ___ with Noah
                          10   2

   in the appearance of each ___ ___ ___ ___ ___ after a storm.
                            3 6

5. Noah was told to make the ark out of gopherwood and to make it 300

   ___ ___ ___ ___ ___ ___ long.
         17

Mystery Answers

God decided to send the flood because of his disappointment with the

___ ___ ___ ___   ___ ___ ___   ___ ___ ___ ___ ___ ___ ___ ___ ___ ___ in the world.
1 2 3 4   5 6 7   8 9 10 11 12 13 14 15 16 17

D. Essay Question

Why did God choose Noah and his family to be saved from the flood?

_____

_____

_____

The Story of the Tower of Babel
Genesis 11: 1-9

When God saved the human race through the three sons of Noah, He clearly revealed His intention of seeing them prosper and multiply to populate the entire world. Noah's sons would become the forefathers of many different **nationalities**. Before the flood all the people had lived in a small section of the world where the Tigris and Euphrates rivers flowed. No one had crossed the mountains on the east or the great desert on the west.

After the flood the descendants of Shem, Ham and Japheth began to move out and inhabit other lands, some crossed the mountains to the east and the north, some went further south into the great plains along the two rivers, and others ventured down into what is now called Africa.

As one group of people were exploring new territory, they found an area between the two great rivers in the land called **Shinar** and decided to stay there. They had learned how to make bricks from the soil of the land so the people began to build houses and cities with this material.

Nimrod, a **descendant** of Ham and a mighty hunter who lived among them easily inspired these people to band together for safety. As they gradually turned away from God, they began to think that they could rule all the people around them. **Nimrod** convinced the people of the need to build a great city. They even planned the erection of a tower that would reach up to the heavens. The tower would make a name for them and would stand as a **monument** to their own glory. With the help of many laborers the tower construction was started. It grew higher and higher until it almost reached the clouds.

God in His great mercy patiently watched from heaven as these misguided people worked to complete the tower. God was saddened and disappointed to see how His people had lost sight of His plan. God wanted to promote a **unity** by creating a variety of **cultures** and governments. But these people wanted to dominate everyone. In their proud ambition they were determined to acknowledge no power above themselves – imagining themselves to be equal to God Himself.

Finally God intervened in a strange and unique way. He caused a confusion of **tongues** among the people. The various groups of workmen began speaking in different languages. They could not understand each other anymore so they couldn't work together in harmony. There was disorder and chaos everywhere. Tempers flared in their frustration. Their tower became known as the **Tower of Babel** stemming from the Hebrew word for "confusion." They gave up on the tower construction and scattered into different parts of the world.

Many separate nations were formed as a direct result of this group of people's attempt to build the Tower of Babel. Friends and families speaking the same languages journeyed out together never to see former friends again. Some traveled north to found the city of **Nineveh**. Another group headed west and settled by the river Nile, where the great empire of **Egypt** was developed. Others traveled northwest to the shores of the Mediterranean Sea, forming the cities of Tyre and Sidon.

Nobody really knows what became of the tower although tradition maintains that it was **demolished** by lightning in a terrible storm. The failure to build a tower to reach heaven teaches us that no man can set himself up as equal to God. Our decisions in life show Him that we understand and welcome the teachings of His son, our Lord Jesus Christ. Sometimes we think that we are in control of everything in our lives and that God is not watching. Like the people of Shinar, we forget that God is very interested in everything we do.

Name: _____ Date: _____

Key Words - The Story of the Tower of Babel

cultures	Egypt	Nimrod	tongues
demolished	monument	Nineveh	Tower of Babel
descendant	nationalities	Shinar	unity

A. Fill in the Blanks

Fill in the blanks with the correct **key words**

1. It has been said that people believe that the Tower of Babel was

   _____ by lightning in a terrible storm.

2. The great empire of _____ was developed by the River Nile.

3. _____ was a descendant of Ham, who was the son of Noah.

4. Since the people of Shinar thought they were equal to God, He

   caused a confusion of _____ among them.

5. The Tower of Babel was to be a _____ to the people's own glory.

B. Matching

Match the **key word** on the left with the correct phrase on the right.

____ 1. Descendant   A. the city where some of the people stayed

____ 2. Demolished   B. different languages

____ 3. Tongues   C. a relative

____ 4. Shinar   D. the land where Nimrod lived

____ 5. Nineveh   E. what happened to the tower

C. A Tower of Words

Fill in the blanks with the best **key word** that answers each question below.

9.

1. __ __ __ __ __

2. __ __ __ __ __ __ __ __

3. __ __ __ __ __ __ __ __ __ __ __

4. __ __ __ __ __

5. __ __ __ __ __ __

6. __ __ __ __ __ __ __ __ __ __ __ __

7. __ __ __ __ __

8. __ __ __ __ __ __ __ __

Across
1. Harmony and agreement
2. A structure to honor someone or something
3. Destroyed
4. Land between the Tigris and Euphrates rivers
5. Descendant of Ham that inspired the people to band together for safety
6. Part of a group of people from the same area
7. Empire by the River Nile
8. The traditions and ways of people in relation to their nationalities

Down
9. The tower the people of Shinar were building became know as this

D. Essay Questions

Explain why the tower was known as the "Tower of Babel."

_____

_____

_____

How do you think God feels when you think you can do things without His help?

_____

_____

The Story of Abraham
Genesis 12 - 19, 25

Few events in the history of our faith are more important than the **covenant** (the promise) God made with Abraham. Abraham (first called Abram) was born on the plains of the great Tigris and Euphrates rivers. He was from Ur, which was to the south of Mt. Ararat where Noah and his sons came out of the Ark and not far from the unfinished Tower of Babel. From this land, Abram eventually moved with his family to Haran.

Abram and his wife **Sarai** found that these new people did not know God. One day, God spoke to Abram and told him to leave his home in Haran and begin a long journey to a distant land God would show him. God told Abram, "I will make of you a great nation and I will bless you; I will make your name great, so that you will be a blessing." From that day on, the Hebrews would be called God's **Chosen People**.

Abram did not fully understand what God was saying or where He intended him to go. But Abram had great faith! He trusted in God even though he could not know where this journey would take him. So, in **obedience** to God, Abram left his home and journeyed into the desert headed for the land of Canaan. When he arrived, God again spoke to Abram saying, "To your **descendants** I will give this land." So to honor and thank God, Abram built an altar and offered sacrifices to Him.

Following the will of God, Abram and Sarai's journey of faith lasted for several years. They traveled from Canaan to Egypt and then back to various parts of Canaan. Abram's family **prospered** so much that eventually he and his nephew Lot separated to claim separate lands for themselves. Abram remained in the land of Canaan while Lot settled in the land on the Jordan plain near the city of Sodom. The people of Sodom were very wicked in the sins they committed against God.

But Abram remained faithful to God and was rewarded with prosperity and the **respect** of the kings of the lands surrounding Canaan. While there, God renewed His promise to Abram by revealing to him, ". . .from where you are, gaze to the north and south, east and west; all the land that you see I will give to you and your descendants . . . I will make your descendants like the dust of the earth." God assured him, "Fear not, Abram! I am your shield; I will make your reward very great."

But Abram found this hard to believe because both he and his wife were over seventy years old and they still did not have children as heirs. God assured him again by saying, "Look up at the sky and count the stars . . . Just so shall your descendents be." Abram put his trust in God and again built an altar to offer sacrifices of praise and thanksgiving to Him. As he did so, God made His covenant, He promised Abram, "To your descendents I will give this land. . ." From this day on, the land of Canaan would be known by the Hebrews as the **Promised Land**.

God's final covenant was made with Abram when he was ninety-nine years old, God called Abram and said, "My covenant with you is this: you are to become the father of a host of nations. No longer shall you be called Abram; your name shall be **Abraham** (which means father) for I am making you the father of a host of nations. . ." God also told Abraham that, from that day on, Sarai should be known as **Sarah** and that she would soon have a son to be named Isaac.

Abraham is remembered as a **Patriarch** of our faith (one of the ancestors to ancient Israel). In fact, many religions in the world today recognize Abraham as an important person in the history of their faith. He was a true servant of God and an example to us of the importance of following God's will every day of our lives.

Name: _____ Date: _____

Key Words - The Story of Abraham

Abraham	covenant	Patriarch	respect
Abram	descendants	Promised Land	Sarah
Chosen People	obedience	prospered	Sarai

A. Crossword

Fill in the blanks with the best **key word(s)** to complete the statements below.

8.
O
1. __ ☐ __ __ __
2. __ __ __ __ ☐ __ __ __ __ __
3. __ __ __ __ __ __ ☐ __ __ __ __
4. __ __ __ __ ☐
5. __ __ __ __ __ __ ☐ __
6. __ __ __ __ __ __ ☐ __
7. __ __ __ __ __ __ ☐ __
E

Across

1. Abraham's original name was _____.

2. God told Abraham that he would give Canaan to his _____ .

3. Canaan is known as the _____ to the Hebrews.

4. Sarah's original name was _____.

5. Abraham _____ as a result of his faithfulness.

6. God made a _____ with Abraham.

7. Abraham was also given the _____ of the kings of the surrounding lands.

Down

8. Abraham and Sarah were rewarded for their _____ to God.

B. True of False

Put the letter T on the line in front of each statement that is true. Put the letter F on the line in front of each statment that is false.

_____ 1. Abram and Sarai did not obey God because they didn't fully understand His plans.

_____ 2. Abram and Sarai moved to new lands when God gave asked them. For their obedience God gave them great prosperity.

B. True of False - continued

_____3. God promised Abram that he and his wife would not have a
       great number of descendants.

_____ 4. The name Abraham means father and was given to Abram
       by God.

C. Matching

Match the **key word(s)** on the left with the correct word or phrase on the right.

_____ 1. Prospered   A. an original ancestor of Israel

_____ 2. Obedience   B. the name that means father

_____ 3. Sarah   C. he was told by God to move

_____ 4. God's chosen people   D. the mother of Isaac

_____ 5. Abraham   E. the Hebrews were also called this

_____ 6. Patriarch   F. doing what you are told

_____ 7. Descendants   G. future generations

_____ 8. Respect   H. opposite of failed

_____ 9. Abram   I. to admire and honor

D. Essay Questions

Why did Abram have a hard time believing God when he was told that his
descendants would be as numerous as the stars in the sky?

_____

_____

_____

Sometimes we are asked to do things that we think are too difficult
or impossible. Has this ever happened to you? Explain.

_____

_____

The Story of Jacob and Esau
Gen. 25-28

When **Isaac,** the child God had promised to Abraham and Sarah, was 40 years old, his father Abraham began to worry that he was not yet married. However, he did not want Isaac to marry one of the Canaanite women because they did not believe in God. So, Abraham sent his trusted servant back to his homeland to find a suitable wife for Isaac. The servant prayed for help to find the right woman. In response to his prayer, God revealed to him a beautiful woman on her way to the well in Haran. When he returned with the woman whose name was **Rebekah,** she became Isaac's wife.

After several years Isaac discovered that Rebekah was unable to have children. Isaac asked God to give them a child. Finally, when Isaac was sixty years old his prayer was answered. Rebekah gave birth to **twins**! God had told Rebekah, "two nations are quarreling in your womb . . . and that the older shall serve the younger." The first baby born had hair all over his body even as a newborn infant. Isaac and Rebekah named him **Esau**. The second baby had a smooth complexion. They named him **Jacob**.

The boys were as different as night and day. Esau, Isaac's favorite, was an outdoorsman and a skillful hunter. Jacob's smooth complexion and enjoyment of domestic activities around the tents made him Rebekah's favorite. While growing up, Jacob knew that Hebrew custom dictated that his brother Esau was entitled to an honored position in the family as well as a double share of the inheritance. This privilege given to every **firstborn** son was known as the **birthright**. Jacob knew how important this birthright was. One day while he was cooking some stew, Jacob saw a chance to trick his older brother. When Esau came home famished and asked for a bowl of stew, Jacob agreed to trade it to Esau for his birthright. Without a thought, to satisfy his hunger, Esau gave Jacob his birthright in exchange for something to eat.

All of this did not matter much until many years later when one day Isaac, who was old and blind, called Esau to his tent. He told him to go out to hunt some food and fix it for him so he could bless him before he died. Rebekah overheard the conversation. Immediately, she called Jacob and told him that his father was about to give Esau the blessing. Rebekah told Jacob to go out and get two choice **kids** (young goats) and bring them to her to cook. Jacob did as she said. When she had the food prepared just the way Isaac liked it, she told Jacob to put on Esau's clothes and to take his father the food. She tied the skins from the goats on Jacob's arms and neck to trick Isaac and make him think these were the arms of Esau, his hairy son. When Isaac heard Jacob's voice he was suspicious. However, the hairy feel of the goat skins

and the smell of Esau's clothes convinced Isaac that this was his oldest son. So he ate the food and gave Jacob the **blessing** intended for Esau.

No sooner had Jacob left Isaac's tent, than Esau came in with the food that he had made. Isaac was very upset when he realized what he had just done. Esau was furious! He exclaimed, "He has **tricked** me out of my inheritance twice! First he took away my birthright and now he has taken away my blessing." Fearing that Esau would kill Jacob, Rebekah persuaded Isaac to let him go to the land of **Haran** to stay with her brother, Laban. Esau soon learned of Jacob's trip. In anger, Esau married two Canaanite women just to get back at his parents.

Through Jacob, God reveals that His plan is often accomplished despite what we think and do. Even though Esau was the rightful heir as the firstborn son, it was Jacob who was chosen by God to be a **Patriarch** of the church.

Name: _____ Date: _____

Key Words - The Story of Jacob and Esau

birthright	firstborn	Jacob	Rebekah
blessing	Haran	kids	tricked
Esau	Isaac	Patriarch	twins

A. Mystery Phrases

Fill in the blanks with the **key words** to complete the statements below.

Across

1. the firstborn son of Isaac and Rebekah
2. Esau gave Jacob his _____ for some stew.
3. Rebekah told Jacob to kill two _____ for her to cook.
4. Rebekah's homeland
5. She helped Jacob deceive Isaac.
6. another word for deceived
7. He wore the skins of two young goats to trick his father.
8. two babies born at the same time
9. Isaac wanted to give his firstborn son a _____ before he died.
10. the father of twins
11. Esau was Isaac's _____ son.

Down

12. Jacob was chosen by God to be a _____ ____ _____ _____.

B. True or False

Put the letter T on the line in front of each statement that is true. Put the letter F on the line in front of each statement that is false.

_____ 1. Isaac and Rebekah were the parents of Abraham.

_____ 2. Esau, the firstborn, was entitled to a double share of inheritance.

_____ 3. Isaac gave a blessing to Esau just before he died.

_____ 4. The main physical difference in the twins was Esau's hairy skin.

_____ 5. Rebekah, fearing for Esau's life, urged him to go to Haran.

C. Matching

Match the **key word** on the left with the correct phrase on the right.

_____ 1. Birthright   A. asking divine care for something

_____ 2. Firstborn   B. a privilege given to the oldest son

_____ 3. Blessing   C. the oldest born in a family

_____ 4. Kids   D. Uncle Laban lived there

_____ 5. Haran   E. Jacob's father

_____ 6. Isaac   F. young goats

D. Essay Questions

Jacob tricked Esau out of his birthright twice. How did he do this? How would you feel if you were Esau?

_____

_____

_____

Since God's plans will be accomplished despite what we do; does that mean we can do whatever we please? Explain.

_____

_____

_____

The Story of Jacob and the 12 Tribes
Genesis 28 - 32

Even though Esau was the first born son of Isaac, God's plan was for his brother **Jacob** to become a Patriarch of His chosen people. To protect Jacob from the wrath of his brother Esau, Jacob's mother Rebekah helped him escape. He traveled into the wilderness bound for the home of Rebekah's brother **Laban** in Mesopotania.

A wonderful thing happened to Jacob on this long journey. One night, as Jacob lay resting on the ground, he began to feel guilty about the **trickery** he and his mother had accomplished against his brother Esau. As it grew dark in the strange place he began to realize that he needed God's protection. Jacob knew that if God's promise to Abraham was to be fulfilled in him he must open his heart to God's will. He knew he could not again take matters into his own hands as he and his mother had done.

As he slept that night, Jacob had a dream of a beautiful **ladder** with angels going up and down. When he opened his heart, God appeared to him. God renewed the promise He had made to Abraham as He told Jacob that "the land on which you are lying I will give to you and your descendants." He promised Jacob that his **descendants** would be "as plentiful as the dust of the earth." God also assured Jacob that He would guide and protect him in the journey just ahead. When Jacob awoke, he exclaimed, "Truly, the LORD is in this spot." Then, Jacob set the stone on which he slept in place as a memorial and proclaimed in thankfulness that he would return to God one-tenth of all worldly things that God would ever give him.

As he approached Laban's house, Jacob came upon some shepherds at a well. When Jacob inquired about his uncle Laban and his well being, they told him that they knew Laban was doing well. In fact, they pointed out that his youngest daughter, **Rachel**, was just now approaching the well. Jacob was immediately taken by Rachel's beauty and grace as he introduced himself to her. When Rachel returned home, she told her father that his nephew Jacob was near. Laban went out to meet Jacob and invited him to come and stay with his family. After about 30 days, Laban employed Jacob to care for his sheep.

During this time Jacob fell in love with Rachel.

In those days, it was customary for a man to offer the father of any woman he intended to marry a payment for that privilege. Jacob did not have anything to offer Laban for Rachel's hand. Instead, he agreed to work in Laban's service for seven years. These years flew by for Jacob, as his love for Rachel was stronger than any concern he had for himself. When the day came for the marriage, Laban tricked Jacob much like Jacob had tricked his brother Esau several years before. Instead of Rachel, Laban offered Jacob his oldest daughter **Leah** as his wife. Jacob protested but finally married Leah only after Laban made him another promise. Laban told Jacob he would give him the hand of his beloved Rachel in a week if he would agree to work in his service for another **seven years**. Reluctantly, Jacob agreed.

During this second seven years, Jacob became the father of eleven sons named Reuben, Simeon, Levi, Judah, Dan, Naphtali, Gad, Asher Issachar, Zebulun and Joseph. After his return to Canaan, Jacob's twelfth son named Benjamin was born. Each of these twelve sons of Jacob grew to become a prince and the head of one of the **twelve tribes** of the Hebrew nation. We know that Jesus was descended from the tribe of Judah.

Six more years passed before Jacob returned with his family to the land of Canaan. As he neared his homeland, he feared that his brother Esau might come to attack him as revenge for tricking him some twenty years before. He made precautions to protect his family and even sent a peace offering to Esau to avoid his wrath. Having done all he could, Jacob went to a quiet place to pray. Again, God communicated to Jacob in a very wonderful way. Suddenly, Jacob was seized by a man, an angel of God, who wrestled with him all night long. Unable to gain the upper hand against Jacob, the angel of God touched Jacob on the leg, making him **lame**. Still, Jacob refused to release his grasp until he received a blessing from the angel. Then the angel asked Jacob, "What is your name?" Jacob told him! The angel said, "Because you have struggled and succeeded against both divine and human beings, you shall no longer be called Jacob (which means the supplanter). Instead, you shall be called **Israel** (which means prince)." From that day forward Jacob would be known as Israel and all his descendants would be known as the **Israelites**.

Key Words - The Story of Jacob and the 12 Tribes

descendants	Jacob	Leah	ladder
Israel	Laban	Rachel	trickery
Israelites	lame	seven years	twelve tribes

A. Word Search - Jacobs Ladder

Jacob's Ladder - Find and mark 11 of the **key word(s)** in the puzzle.

						L	A	S	T		
						L	E	E	W		
						A	R	T	E		
						E	T	I	L		
		R	A	C	L	R	L	L	V		
		A	A	E	I	S	E	A	E		
		C	A	C	O	I	A	E	T		
		H	K	E	M	A	L	R	R		
J	S	E	V	E	N	Y	E	A	R	S	I
T	A	C	R	L	K	E	B	R	Y	I	B
R	I	Y	B	O	C	A	J	W	T	W	E
D	E	S	C	E	N	D	A	N	T	S	S

B. Fill in the Blanks

Fill in the correct **key word(s)** in the following statements. Then unscramble the letters in the boxes to reveal the answer to the bonus question.

1. Esau's younger brother __ ☐ __ __ __ fled to the home of his

   uncle ☐ __ __ __ __.

2. Jacob worked for ☐ __ __ __ __ __ __ __ __ __ for his uncle so he could

   marry his daughter ☐ __ __ __ __ __ but Laban tricked him and gave him

   the hand of __ ☐ __ __ instead.

3. Each of Jacob's sons later became a leader of one of the __ __ __ __ __ __

   __ __ ☐ __ __ __.

   Bonus Question: What was Jacob's name changed to? __ __ __ __ __ __

C. True or False

Put the letter T on the line in front of each statement that is true. Put the letter F on the line in front of each statement that is false.

_____ 1. Jacob felt guilty about tricking his brother Esau.

_____ 2. Jacob was told in his dream that his descendants would be "as plentiful as the dust of the earth."

_____ 3. On the spot where Jacob slept he built a temple to praise God.

_____ 4. Jacob paid 30 pieces of silver for the hand of Rachel.

_____ 5. Because Jacob was afraid Esau might still be mad when he went back home, he sent a peace offering to him.

_____ 6. While Jacob wrestled with an angel of God he was made lame.

_____ 7. Descendents of Jacob are known as Israelites because his name was changed to Israel by his father Isaac.

D. Essay Questions

What tribe of Israel did Jesus' family belong to?   Name one other Biblical character that was also a member of this family.

_____

_____

_____

_____

Jacob proclaimed to God that he would return to God one tenth of all worldly things that God would give him. Today we call this "tithing." Why is giving so important?

_____

_____

_____

_____

The Story of Joseph
Genesis 37 - 46

Of Israel's (once known as Jacob) twelve sons, his favorite was Joseph. Joseph, like his younger brother Benjamin, was the son of Rachel, the wife Jacob had loved since the first day he met her. Joseph's father was so fond of him, that he made him a beautiful **coat of many colors**. Joseph wore his coat with pride knowing that it represented the special love his father had for him.

Joseph's older brothers were **jealous** of him. To them, this younger brother was a threat. Their jealousy grew even stronger when they saw that God had given Joseph a unique talent of interpreting dreams. Then, when Joseph inter-

preted two of his dreams to mean that he would one day be the greatest of the brothers in the eyes of God, their jealousy turned to hatred. His brothers seized an opportunity to do away with Joseph at a place called Dothan. Joseph's father had sent him out to check on his brothers. When they saw him coming (recognizing his colorful coat), some of them wanted to kill Joseph and throw his body into a deep well. But **Reuben**, his oldest brother, convinced them to simply throw him in the well and leave him to die. Reuben planned to return and rescue him later.

When a band of traders headed for Egypt came by, **Judah**, another brother saw an opportunity to get rid of Joseph without killing him. He convinced all the

others to sell Joseph as a slave to this band of traders. So, they sold Joseph to them for 20 pieces of silver. Once in Egypt, Joseph was sold to **Potiphar** the chief **steward** of Pharaoh. He became a dedicated servant in Potiphar's house. In fact, Potiphar was so pleased with Joseph that he put him in charge of his own household and all of his possessions. God blessed Potiphar's house for Joseph's sake. Even when Joseph was thrown into prison after being falsely accused by Potiphar's wife, Joseph continued to prosper. Through God's blessing, Joseph was treated kindly by the chief jailer and put in charge of all of the prisoners. While in jail, Joseph again used his talent of **interpreting** dreams for two of Pharaoh's imprisoned servants. Two years passed before Joseph's talent was remembered as he was called before Pharaoh to interpret his dreams. None of Pharaoh's sages or magicians could tell him what they meant.

After listening to Pharaoh's explanation of two dreams, Joseph told him that God would provide the answer to him. With God's help, Joseph told Pharaoh that his dreams meant that Egypt was soon to see seven years of plenty followed by seven years of famine. **Pharaoh** was so impressed with Joseph that he put him in charge of all of the affairs of Egypt to see the country through these fourteen years. Just as Joseph had predicted, the times of plenty and **famine** came to pass. But, because of Joseph's stewardship of the land, Egypt not only survived the years of famine but had surplus food to sell to other nations.

After learning of this abundance, Jacob sent all of his sons except Benjamin into Egypt to buy food and provisions for their families in Israel. The ten brothers ended up at the feet of Joseph to beg for food (just as Joseph's first dream many years before had predicted). Although Joseph recognized his brothers, the ten brothers did not recognize him. After returning a second time they discovered that Joseph was their brother. Through all this time, Joseph never held a grudge against his brothers. He even got Pharaoh's permission to allow his father Jacob and all his descendants to move into the land of **Goshen**, the most fertile land in Egypt to be saved from the famine in Canaan.

The Israelites prospered in **Egypt** for over four hundred years because of God's blessing on His faithful servant Joseph. We again learn in this story that God's divine plan is often accomplished despite human failings. Joseph's **forgiveness** of all those who ever wronged him (including his own brothers) and his commitment to always honor God's wishes is a powerful lesson for us of how to handle challenges and adversity in our daily lives.

Name: _____ Date: _____

Key Words - The Story of Joseph

coat of many colors   forgiveness   jealous   Potiphar
Egypt   Goshen   Judah   Reuben
famine   interpret   Pharaoh   steward

A. Joseph's Coat Puzzle

Fill in the blanks with the key word(s) to complete the statements below.

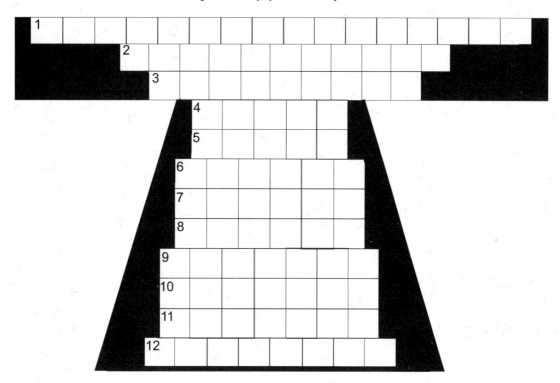

1. Joseph's coat

2. Joseph offered _____ to everyone who wronged him.

3. Joseph had a God-given talent to _____ dreams.

4. Joseph's brother who wanted to sell him as a slave to a band of traders

5. the country where the band of traders sold Joseph

6. a time of failed crops and food shortages

7. Joseph's brother who wanted to throw him into a well

8. the area of Egypt given to Jacob and his family by Pharaoh

9. the ruler of Egypt whose dreams Joseph interpreted

10. a servant who supervises his owner's property

11. Joseph's brothers were so _____ of him they wanted to kill him.

12. He was Pharaoh's chief steward.

B. Scrambled Words

Unscramble the **key word(s)** and fill in the blank(s) to complete each sentence.

1. Joseph's father Jacob loved him so much that he made him a _____

   ___ _____ _____. MTOLCONOFYRSAOCA

2. Joseph's coat made his brothers _____. LEASOUJ

3. _____ NEBEUR convinced the brothers to throw Joseph into a well.

4. Once Joseph arrived in _____ PYGTE, _____ HAAORPHS

   chief _____ TWESRAD _____ THROPAIP

   bought Joseph to work as a servant in his house.

5. When Pharaoh called on Joseph to _____ PRETETRIN

   his dreams, Joseph told him that there would be seven years of plenty

   followed by seven years of _____ INFEMA.

6. In addition to the _____ GNFIEOVSRES

   Joseph offered his brothers he asked Pharaoh to let his family live in the

   land of _____ SHEONG.

C. Essay Questions

Joseph forgave everyone who wronged him because he trusted that God was still watching over him even in bad situations. Is there someone that you need to forgive? Why is it hard to forgive sometimes?

_____

_____

_____

Do you believe that God is watching over you? Give one example.

_____

_____

_____

The Story of Moses and the Burning Bush
Exodus 3; 4:1-17

One day while Moses was leading the flock of his father-in-law, Jethro, across the desert; he came to **Mount Horeb**, called the mountain of God. There he noticed a strange and wonderful sight. He saw a burning bush. He was fascinated because the bush was on fire but it did not burn up. He decided to take a closer look at it. When he got closer, he heard the voice of God call him by name, "Moses! Moses!"

Moses answered, "Here I am." God said to him, "Come no nearer! Remove the sandals from your feet, for the place where you stand is holy ground. I am the God of your father, the God of Abraham, the God of Isaac, the God of Jacob." Moses covered his face at once because he was too afraid to look at God. But the Lord told him "Come, now! I will send you to **Pharaoh** to lead my people, the **Israelites**, out of Egypt."

But Moses was not sure why God had chosen him. He asked God, "Who am I that I should go to Pharaoh and lead the Israelites out of Egypt?" God answered, "I will be with you; and this shall be your proof that it is I who have sent you; when you bring My people out, you will worship God on this very mountain." But Moses said to God, "When I go to the Israelites, [who shall I say sent me]?" God replied, "I am who am,. . . Tell the Israelites; **I AM** sent me to you. . . . The God of your fathers, the God of Abraham, the God of Isaac, the God of Jacob, has sent Me to you."

God then told Moses to tell the Israelite elders that He had appeared to Moses because He was concerned about the way they are being treated. God also told him that He had decided to lead them out of the misery of Egypt and into the land of **Canaan**, the prosperous land flowing with milk and honey that I had promised them long ago.

God also gave him a message for Pharaoh telling him to free the Hebrew people from their bondage. God knew that the king would not allow the Hebrews to leave unless he was forced, so God told Moses, "I will stretch out My hand . . . and smite Egypt by doing all kinds of wondrous deeds there. After that he will send you away."

In spite of all these wonderful promises from God, Moses still didn't think that he was **qualified** to do the job. To encourage him, the Lord gave him two special **signs** or miracles. First, God turned Moses' staff into a serpent and back into a staff. Then God made Moses' hand diseased with **leprosy** and, in an instant, completely healed it.

Even after these signs, Moses worried that his limited **vocabulary** and his speech handicap would make him a very poor spokesman for God and His people. At this point, God lost His patience with Moses for his lack of faith and for suggesting that someone else go in his place. God decided to send Moses' brother **Aaron**, along to speak for him. Even while they were still talking, the Lord caused Aaron to go out to the wilderness to seek Moses. God told Moses that He would teach both him and Aaron what to say and do. Finally, Moses accepted God's mission.

Moses did not see himself as a spokesman or a leader but God selected him to free His chosen people. God provided everything necessary to succeed in the job He gave Moses, but Moses had to choose to trust and obey God.

Name: _____   Date: _____

Worksheet #8

Key Words - The Story of Moses and the Burning Bush

Aaron	I AM	Moses	qualified
bondage	Israelites	Mount Horeb	signs
Canaan	leprosy	Pharaoh	vocabulary

A. Secret Code
Using the key below, decipher the code and fill in the blanks.

○ M   ⊙ E   ＼ N   ⊘ S

△ C   ＋ I   ＊ H

□ A   ⊠ P   ▽ L

✕ R   ／ O   ⊞ T

1. _____
○／○○⊙○

2. _____
□□✕／＼

3. _____
⊠＊□✕□／＊

4. _____
＋ □○

5. _____
＋⊘✕□⊙▽＋⊞○⊙○

6. _____
△□＼□□＼

B. Fill in the Blanks
Fill in the blanks with the correct **key word(s)**

1. God asked Moses to go to _____ to ask him to release the
   _____.

2. The people that Moses was to lead out of Egypt were being held in
   _____.

3. Moses was tending sheep when he came to _____ _____ where
   he saw a burning bush.

4. Moses didn't believe that he was _____ to lead God's people
   since he had a poor _____.

5. Finally, God decided to send _____ with Moses to speak for him.

© 2000 Fireside Bible Publishers. May not be reproduced without the written permission of the publisher.

C. Matching

Match the **key word** on the left with the correct phrase or word on the right.

_____ 1. Leprosy   A. being held captive

_____ 2. Signs   B. the land of milk & honey

_____ 3. Bondage   C. a disease that affects the skin

_____ 4. Vocabulary   D. miracles

_____ 5. Canaan   E. a group of words used by a person

_____ 6. Qualified   F. being able to do something well

D. Essay Questions

What were the signs that God gave Moses to encourage him?

_____

_____

_____

_____

Have your ever been asked to do something that you didn't feel qualified or able to do? Explain.

_____

_____

_____

How would you respond to God if He asked you to do something for him?

_____

_____

The Story of the Plagues on Egypt
Exodus 4:18 - 15:1

In answer to God's call from the burning bush on Mt. Horeb, Moses and his brother Aaron returned to Egypt. God had heard the **pleas** of His chosen people who were suffering at the hands of the Egyptians. In His infinite mercy, He sent Moses (who was eighty years old) back to free them from bondage and to lead them out of Egypt and into the Promised Land.

But it would not be easy. When Moses first commanded Pharaoh in the name of God to, "Let My people go," God allowed Pharaoh's heart to be hardened. As a result, **Pharaoh** went to the taskmasters and demanded even more work out of his Hebrew slaves. Now, instead of just forcing them to make bricks, he quit providing them the straw to do so. Yet, he required the same amount of bricks to be made. The Israelites suffered in these hot brickyards with barely enough food to eat or water to drink.

The Hebrew foremen were very upset at **Moses** for this. They asked Moses why he had put them in such bad favor with Pharaoh. In response, Moses asked God why he had been sent on such a difficult mission. God reassured Moses. He told him that Pharaoh would be "forced by My mighty hand" to send the Israelites away. God told Moses to tell the Israelites that He was going to honor the **covenant** (the promise) He had made with Abraham. He told Moses that He was going to use him as His **instrument** to set the Hebrew people free.

To do this, God told Moses, "I will lay My hand on Egypt and by great acts of judgment convince Pharaoh to set the Israelites free." With this promise, Moses returned again and again to Pharaoh with God's demand, "Let My people go to worship Me in the desert."

But Pharaoh did not listen. Each time Pharaoh said "No." Then God brought terrible **plagues** on Egypt. As a result of his refusal to obey God, Pharaoh and Egypt suffered through nine different plaques. They included:

1) the river turning to blood; 2) a plague of frogs; 3) a plague of gnats; 4) a plague of flies; 5) a plague of **pestilence** or sickness and death of their animals; 6) a plague of boils; 7) a plague of hail; 8) a plague of **locusts**; 9) a plague of darkness.

Even after the nine plagues, Pharaoh refused to let the Israelites and their flocks go. So God told Moses He would **inflict** one final plague on Egypt more terrible than all the previous plagues combined. He instructed Moses to tell Pharaoh that if he did not let the Israelites go, the firstborn child of every man and beast in Egypt would die. Only the Israelites would be spared this terrible punishment. Still Pharaoh refused.

God instructed Moses to prepare the Israelites for this most important night in a very special way. Moses told the Hebrew people that they should prepare a special **Passover** meal of lamb, unleavened bread and bitter herbs. They were to dress prepared to leave quickly. Moses also told them to mark the doorposts and **lintel** (the top of the door frame) of each house using the blood from the Passover lamb. When the angel of death saw the blood markings he would "pass over" that house. Lastly, God told the chosen people that this night should always be remembered. This celebration was one of the reasons Jesus went to Jerusalem a few days before He died. That is why Jesus is referred to as the **Lamb of God**.

Then, the angel of death came to Egypt on that first Passover night. Every firstborn, both man and animal, in the land was slain. Even the Pharaoh's son died. But, in His mercy, God saved all of Israel because of their faith in Him. When Pharaoh witnessed the power of God, he called Moses in the middle of the night and set the Israelites free!

Key Words - The Story of the Plagues on Egypt

covenant	Lamb of God	Moses	Pharaoh
inflict	lintel	Passover	plagues
instrument	locusts	pestilence	pleas

A. Hailstone Scramble

Unscramble the letters to form the **key words** in the blanks below

_____ _____ _____ _____

_____ _____ _____ _____

B. Matching

Match the **key word(s)** on the left with the word or phrase on the right.

1. ____ Moses   A. an event to remember freedom from Egypt
2. ____ Pharaoh   B. God's afflictions on Egypt
3. ____ Passover   C. sickness of animals
4. ____ Pleas   D. grasshoppers
5. ____ Pestilence   E. to make happen, bring about
6. ____ Plagues   F. Jesus is called this
7. ____ Instrument   G. the person who delivered God's message
8. ____ Inflict   H. appeals
9. ____ Covenant   I. he held the Israelites captive
10. ____ Lintel   J. something used to do a task
11. ____ Locusts   K. a promise
12. ____ Lamb of God   L. top of the door frame

C. The Pyramid of Plagues

Fill in the appropriate plague in the pyramid below.

10. death of
    every

f_____

8.

l_____

9.

d_____

5.

p_____
of animals

6.

b_____

7.

h_____

1. water turned
   to

b_____

2.

f_____

3.

g_____

4.

f_____

D. Essay Questions

What did the Hebrew people call it when the angel of God saved their firstborn?

_____

_____

_____

_____

Why was celebrating this event so important to Jesus?

_____

_____

_____

The Story of the Red Sea
Exodus 12:37 - 15:1

On the night that Pharaoh set the Israelites free, Moses led over **600,000 men** and their families out of Egypt as they headed for the Promised Land. There may have been as many as two million people altogether counting the women and children. It was the greatest **exodus** of people, animals and belongings the world had ever seen. It was also a surprise to many of God's chosen people. They even had to take **unleavened bread** with them to eat for they didn't have time to prepare their bread as usual.

To avoid confronting the Philistines, the Israelites set out on a path through the uncharted wilderness leading them toward the banks of the **Red Sea**. God told Moses how the Israelites should celebrate the Passover. And through Moses, God told the Israelites how that they should always remember how He delivered them from the hands of the Egyptians. The Israelites were also instructed that the oldest child in every family should be **dedicated** to God. This would be a lasting reminder of God's saving of the firstborn of the Israelites on the night when the firstborn in Egypt were taken by death.

In Egypt, Pharaoh's heart had hardened again. He began to think about what he had lost. Remember, the Hebrews were Pharaoh's entire workforce. He was very sorry that he had let them go. Pharaoh and his men knew the Israelites were in the wilderness and trapped between the mountains and the Red Sea. He was determined to recapture them and bring them back to Egypt. He organized a great force to go after them. He called for his own chariot, and for six hundred **chariots** of his army; with many  squadrons of horsemen, and with thousands of his bravest soldiers.

Soon the Israelites heard the rumblings of the Egyptian's chariot wheels and the thundering of their horses' hoofs. They knew that the heart of Pharaoh was filled with hatred, and that he must be coming after them. But where could they go to escape? There were mountains on both sides of them and a powerful sea in front of them. Many of the Hebrews thought they might die in this trap. They cried to Moses, "Far better for us to be the slaves of the Egyptians than to die in the desert."

Moses said, "Fear not, . . . you will see the **victory** the LORD will win for you today!" Then, God sent a great dark column of cloud to stop the Egyptian advance and commanded Moses to lift his staff out over the waters of the Red Sea. Suddenly, the sea parted and a swift wind blew all night drying the sea floor. The Israelites marched into the midst of the sea on dry land with a **wall of water** on the left and a wall of water on the right. When they were nearly across, God lifted the column of cloud and Pharaoh and his entire Egyptian army foolishly chased the Hebrews into the Sea.

From the other side of the Red Sea Moses looked back and saw that God had thrown Pharaoh's army into **chaos** on the dry floor of the sea. Their chariot wheels became jammed and their men and horses began to panic. When the Egyptians realized that their problems were caused by an act of the God of Israel, they tried to go back but it was too late. Before they could return to the safety of the river bank, God commanded Moses to lift his **staff** toward the Egyptians. The mighty walls of water came rushing down upon them, drowning all of the Egyptain army.

The Israelites knew in this wonderful event that God had truly blessed them. They also knew that He was with them through His **faithful servant** Moses. Therefore, once they reached safety, Moses and the Israelites sang a song in praise to God which began: "I will sing to the LORD, for he is gloriously triumphant; horse and chariot he has cast into the sea."

Name: _____ Date: _____

Key Words - The Story of the Red Sea

600,000 men	dedicated	Moses	unleavened bread
chaos	exodus	Red Sea	victory
chariots	faithful servant	staff	wall of water

A. Cross – A – Clue

Put 10 of the 12 **key words** into the cross-a-clue grid. Hint: Count the number of letters in each word. The words all read left to right or top to bottom.

B. Matching

Match the **key word(s)** on the left with the correct word or phrase on the right.

_____1. Chaos   A. success

_____ 2. Staff   B. a large group leaving

_____ 3. Dedicated   C. a stick used for support

_____ 4. Exodus   D. confusion and disorder

_____ 5. Victory   E. Moses was this

_____ 6. Faithful servant   F. set apart or saved for a special purpose

C. Fill in the Blanks

Fill in the blank(s) with the correct answer from the answer bank. Then put the letters of the answers in the blanks below to reveal the mystery word.

ANSWER BANK

A = 600,000 men   I = unleavened bread
E = wall of water   S = victory
L = 600 chariots   R = faithful servant
I = chaos   T = exodus
E = staff   S = dedicated

1. God's chosen people had to take _____ with them to eat.

2. Moses told the people that God would lead them to _____.

3. Moses was God's _____ _____.

4. Moses led _____ _____ and their families out of Egypt.

5. The people marched into the Red Sea on dry land with a _____ _____ _____ on each side of them.

6. Pharaoh chased the Isrealites with his _____ _____ and his army.

7. Pharaoh's army was in _____ on the "dry' sea floor.

8. Moses led the largest _____ of people the world had ever seen.

9. Moses lifted his _____ out over the waters and they parted.

10. The people _____ their firstborn children to God.

Mystery word ___ ___ ___ ___ ___ ___ ___ ___ ___ ___
                 1   2   3   4   5   6   7   8   9 10

D. Essay Questions

Why did God want the oldest child of each family dedicated to Him?

_____

_____

_____

Why is water so important in this story and in the practice of our Catholic faith?

_____

_____

_____

The Story of Manna in the Desert
Exodus 15: 23-37; 16

Following the great triumph over their enemies in the miraculous crossing of the Red Sea, there was a season of rejoicing in the camp of Israel. Guided by a pillar of cloud by day and a pillar of fire by night, the Israelites turned into the great desert, toward the place where **Moses** had seen the burning bush.

After traveling for three days they came to **Mara**, a place where there were springs of water. The **Israelites** forgot the mercies and power of God, and began murmuring against Moses because of the bitterness of the water. Then the Lord directed Moses to find a certain piece of wood and to throw it into the water. Immediately, the water became pure and good to drink. Moses reminded the people that all would go well with them if they would only trust in the Lord and obey His commandments.

The children of Israel then journeyed to a place called **Elim**, a beautiful valley with twelve fountains of water and seventy palm trees. They camped for several months before resuming their journey. As they traveled deeper into the desert, they came into what was known as the Desert of Sin between Elim and Mt. Sinai. In the months since leaving **Egypt**, the Israelites had used up most of their food supplies. The sheep and cattle that they brought with them from Egypt had to be kept for making offerings to God, and for building flocks and herds in their new home. So, the people began to wonder where they would find food. Fear and panic spread among them, and they worried that they might even starve to death. They remembered that even during the captivity and hardships suffered in Egypt they had never gone hungry. In their desperation the people murmured against Moses and **Aaron** and even longed to return to their old life of slavery in Egypt.

The Lord knew that these complaints against His servants were really complaints

Gathering the Manna

against Him, yet He looked with tender mercy upon His people. So, He told Moses of His plan to supply Israel with meat in the evening and bread in the morning. He declared that He would send food from heaven down like rain. The elders and leaders of each tribe announced these promises of God to the people of Israel and they were called to worship. In the evening, as they looked toward the wilderness in the east, the glory of the Lord shone in the clouds. As the sun sank on the horizon the Lord caused great flocks of **quail** to descend on their camp; so many that the ground was covered with them. There was meat enough for everyone.

When the people awoke the next morning and looked around them, they saw that the ground was covered with small flakes, white like frost, and sparkling in the dew like diamonds. They were so amazed that they shouted, "**Manna**! Manna!" which means, "What is it?"

Moses explained to them that this was the bread which the Lord had promised to send and that they should go out and gather just enough of it to last them for one day. This wonderful supply of food was to be given by the Lord every morning except the Sabbath, so on the sixth day of each week the people were to gather a double portion.

God sent manna as a free gift of Divine grace, but the people had to use their own strength in gathering it and their own skill in preparing it in various ways. God fed them, but they had to work to satisfy their hunger. Early each morning, before the sun could melt it, the people gathered an **omer** of manna for each person as directed by Moses. Manna was a nourishing food that tasted like wafers and honey.

Whenever one of the Israelites disobeyed the Lord's command and took more than he needed, it would become rotten and wormy before it could be eaten. Those who failed to gather a double portion on the sixth day of the week found that there was no manna to be had on the Sabbath. For their disobedience the Israelites had to go without food for one day.

Moses ordered Aaron to keep an omer of Manna in an **urn** as a memorial of God's wonderful providence in feeding Israel during the long **exile** of forty years in the desert. Later this urn of manna was placed in the sacred **Ark** of the Covenant. It was a valuable reminder to future generations of God's power to provide for His people in need.

Name: _____ Date: _____

Key Words - The Story of Manna in the Desert

Aaron	Elim	manna	omer
Ark	exile	Mara	quail
Egypt	Israelites	Moses	urn

A. Word Search

Find and circle the 12 **key words** in the puzzle below.

```
I   C   N   O   R   A   A   H   T   J
B   S   E   X   I   L   E   P   O   A
S   R   R   N   F   R   Y   Q   R   N
A   V   R   A   Z   G   N   K   S   N
B   O   T   R   E   S   E   D   Z   A
B   L   W   Q   G   L   L   B   F   M
A   M   U   M   U   R   I   N   G   O
T   X   R   A   R   A   M   T   L   S
H   O   N   E   Y   V   C   H   E   E
O   M   E   R   L   I   A   U   Q   S
```

B. Fill in the Blanks

Fill in the blanks with the **key words** to complete the statements below.

1. God provided the Israelites _____ for food in the evening.

2. Moses was assisted by his brother _____ in leading the Israelites.

3. The Israelites spent forty years in _____ in the desert wilderness.

4. Moses instructed Aaron to save an _____ of manna as a testimony to future generations.

5. _____ was the place where there were springs of bitter water.

6. There were 70 palm trees in the valley at _____.

7. Every day except the Sabbath the Israelites were instructed to gather the _____.

8. The Israelites were freed from _____ just before their exile in the desert.

C. Matching

Match the **key word** on the left with the correct phrase on the right.

____ 1. Manna   A. the place where Aaron stored the urn of manna

____ 2. Desert   B. the small flakes that fed the Israelites in the desert

____ 3. Moses   C. the period when the Israelites were in the desert

____ 4. Ark   D. a stone jar used to store water and food

____ 5. Mara   E. he led the Israelites out of slavery in Egypt

____ 6. Israelites   F. the place where the Israelites spent 40 years in exile

____ 7. Exile   G. the place where the water was bitter and unfit to drink

____ 8. Urn   H. the name given to the chosen people of God

D. Essay Questions

The Israelites often complained when they faced challenges in the desert. Have you ever reacted the same way to challenges? Explain.

_____

_____

_____

What lesson can we learn from God's response to the Israelites?

_____

_____

_____

Like the manna from heaven, what gift does God give us as spiritual food?

_____

_____

_____

The Story of the Ten Commandments
Exodus 19, 20

After being sustained in the wilderness by God's blessing of manna from heaven, the Israelites camped for nearly a year on the plain before the great mountain of Sinai. Here, through Moses, God revealed many rules for the domestic, social, and religious life of His people. Full instructions were given for the elaborate system of worship and priestly sacrifices. The tabernacle was built and the furnishings and a portable altar were made. Many other important customs were founded. However, no message was more important than God's **proclamation** of the **Ten Commandments**.

When Moses first went up to the mountain God said, "Tell the Israelites . . . if you [listen] to My voice and keep My **covenant**, you shall be My special possession, dearer to Me than all other people . . . You shall be to Me a kingdom of priests, a holy nation." When Moses returned and told the people this they replied, "Everything the LORD has said, we will do."

Moses returned to the top of **Mount Sinai**. God told him to return to the people again and tell them to wash themselves and their garments and to prepare for the third day. They were cautioned that God was about to speak, and that under the penalty of immediate death, they must not touch the foot of the mountain, or go beyond the bounds already set for them by the great **column of smoke** and fire God would create.

Then, on the morning of the **third day**, there were great claps of thunder and lightning brighter than the sun. Trumpet blasts filled the air around the entire mountain. With this announcement, God called Moses to the mountaintop for the third time and told him to warn the people that they must not try to come forward to see Him. God told Moses that only he and his brother Aaron should return the next time.

When Moses and Aaron returned, God announced in words which all could hear and understand, "I, the LORD am Your God, who brought you out of the land of Egypt, that place of slavery." Then God spoke to Moses the Ten Commandments. Three million Israelites heard them word for word (in their own language).

God said from the top of Mount Sinai:

You shall not have other gods besides Me.

You shall not take the name of the LORD your God, in **vain**.

Remember to keep holy the **Sabbath Day**.

Honor your father and your mother.

You shall not kill.

You shall not commit adultery.

You shall not steal.

You shall not **bear false witness** against your neighbor.

You shall not covet your neighbor's [belongings].

You shall not **covet** your neighbor's wife.

These Ten Commandments were written by the finger of God on two **stone tablets** and brought down from the mountain by Moses.

Upon hearing the voice of God, the Israelites were overcome with terror.

They said to Moses, "You speak to us, and we will listen; but let not God speak to us, or we shall die." But Moses told the Israelites "Do not be afraid, for God has come to you only to test you and put his fear upon you, lest you should sin."

The Ten Commandments are laws that tell us to love, honor and respect God and each other. Jesus summed them up best in the **Sermon on the Mount** when He said, "Love the Lord, your God, with all your heart," and "Love your neighbor as yourself." In these words Jesus reveals that His message of love for God and each other, is the same message that Moses received from God the Father on Mount Sinai.

Key Words - The Story of the Ten Commandments

bear false witness	Mount Sinai	stone tablets
column of smoke	proclamation	Ten Commandments
covenant	Sabbath Day	third day
covet	Sermon on the Mount	vain

A. Ten Commandments Scramble

The letters in each vertical column go into the squares directly below them, (but not necessarily in the same order). A black square indicates the end of a word. When you have placed all the letters in their correct squares you will find the primary words of each of the 10 Commandments. Each puzzle contains 2 of the Commandments. In the circle in front of each puzzle write the correct number of the Commandments from 1-10.

H	E	Y	E	H	O	Y	R	U	R	O	F	A	E	E	E	R	T	H	N	D	S	M	B	B	H	E	H
D	A	M	O	M	B	E	O		T			K	T	H	P		A	E			A	O	T	A	T	R	
R	O	N		R		L	Y																				

Y	O	I	G	S	B	A	R	L		N	E	T	O	N	T	E	E	G	S	Y	O	U	R
Y	O	U		H	H	O	L	L		B	O	T		S	G	I	N	T					
N	E	U		S	H	A	L	S		N	O	L		C	O	V	A	L					

B	E	U	I		D	H	A	L	L	E	N	A	V	E	K	I		O	L	O	T	H	E	R		G	O	D	S
Y	O	S			S	H	S	L	L		H	O	T			N	L												
Y	O	U			S	E	A		M																				

Y	F	U	G	S	D	A	I	L		V	O	I	N	C	A	M	E	I	T	H	E	D	U	L	M	E	R	Y
Y	O	U		O	H	A	L	N		N	O	T		T	O	K	M	T		A		N	A	T	E			
O	O			S	H		L	L		N	A	T																

W	I	U	N	E	B	A	L	A	G	N	I	T	E	C	E	V	E	U	F	A	L	S	E	G	H	B	O	R
Y	E	U	G	H	H	S	L	L		N	I	N	S	T	O	Y	R	T	R	Y	O	E	R					
Y	O	I		S	S	A	R	L		A	O	T		B		A	O				N	U	I					
N	O	T		S	H	O		S		W	O	F																

B. Matching

Match the **key word(s)** on the left with the correct word or phrase on the right.

_____ 1. Proclamation   A. promise

_____ 2. Covenant   B. without respect

_____ 3. Vain   C. declaration

_____ 4. Sabbath Day   D. day of worship

_____ 5. Covet   E. commandments written on this

_____ 6. Bear false witness   F. want what someone else has

_____ 7. Stone tablets   G. to lie

C. True or False

Put the letter T on the line in front of each statement that is true. Put the letter F on the line in front of each statement that is false.

_____ 1. Moses was listening to the Sermon on the Mount when he was given the Ten Commandments.

_____ 2. It was on top of Mount Sinai that Moses heard God speak to him.

_____ 3. Moses was called by God several times to receive rules to live and worship by. The third day God gave him the Ten Commandments.

_____ 4. Jesus best summed up how to live the Ten Commandments in His Sermon on the Mount.

_____ 5. God wrote the commandments on the stone tablets with His finger.

_____ 6. Only Moses and Aaron heard God's voice.

D. Essay Questions

What does it mean to take the Lord's name in vain?

_____

_____

_____

How is the "Golden Rule," which states that we should treat others like we would like to be treated, similar to the Ten Commandments?

_____

_____

_____

The Story of Joshua and the Battle of Jericho
Joshua 3-6

After the Hebrews fled Egypt they spent **forty years** in the wilderness because of their disobedience to God. Finally they arrived at the Jordan River, the boundary of Canaan, "the land flowing with milk and honey." This is the same land that had been promised by God to the patriarchs Abraham, Isaac, and Jacob as well as to Moses. Even though he was about to die, God had promised Moses that He would allow him to see the "Promised Land" from Mount Nebo. Moses

appointed **Joshua**, the son of Nun to be his successor. Moses reviewed God's "Ten Commandments" with the people and then wrote them out on a scroll to be kept with the **Ark of the Covenant**. Before he died, Moses called one last assembly with the entire nation and sang them a song and gave them a final blessing.

After a thirty day mourning period on the plains of Moab, God spoke to Joshua telling him to get the people ready to cross the **Jordan River** and take possession of the land of Canaan. He shared God's plan with the leaders of the twelve tribes so that they could pass it on to their people.

Joshua had learned from the two spies he secretly sent out that the citizens of **Jericho** were so afraid of the Israelites that they had shut themselves inside the walled city. They had heard the reports of how God dealt with enemies of His chosen people. So Joshua, following God's instructions, ordered that the Ark would lead the people across the Jordan. Once again, just like at the Red Sea, the waters were held back by the hand of God as the people crossed the riverbed on dry ground. The priests carrying the Ark remained motionless in the Jordan while the whole nation crossed the riverbed. There were so many people that it took a long time!

After everyone had safely arrived on the other side, Joshua commanded the people to choose twelve men, one from each of the **twelve tribes** to select a  stone from the riverbed in front of the priests holding the Ark and carry it back to him. From the stones they built a **monument** as a memorial of God's miraculous help in crossing the Jordan River. Joshua also had twelve other stones placed in the bed of the river on the spot where the priests stood holding the Ark. As soon as these stones were placed, Joshua called the priests to come out of the river. Then, when they were safely on the bank, the walls of water came together and river began to flow.

The Israelites named the place where they camped **Gilgal** meaning "circle of standing stones" and celebrated the Passover meal there. The next day they ate the produce of this new land for the first time making a meal of unleavened bread and parched grain. That day the manna disappeared! God had only supplied it while it was necessary to keep His chosen people alive.

The Lord gave instructions for the defeat of Jericho. Joshua obeyed! The Israelites also obeyed! Handpicked troops marched in front of seven priests blowing **rams' horns**. Behind them came the priests carrying the Ark followed by the rear guard soldiers and the rest of the people. Each day for six days they marched around the walled city of Jericho one time.   On the **seventh day**, they began early in the morning and marched around the city seven times. Afer the seventh time around, Joshua signaled for the priests to blow their horns again and for all the people to shout. The walls just **collapsed**! They captured the city and all of the treasures in it.

Because Joshua had trusted and **obeyed** the Lord, he was blessed with victories throughout his lifetime. The Israelites realized that he was truly chosen by God.

Name: _____ Date: _____

Key Words - The Story of Joshua and the Battle of Jericho

Ark of the Covenant	Gilgal	Joshua	rams' horns
collapsed	Jericho	monument	seventh day
forty years	Jordan River	obeyed	twelve tribes

A. Monument of Words

Unscramble the letters (except the one in the box) to find the answer to each statement. Then unscramble the boxed letters to reveal the mystery word.

1. (AOHJU[E]S) __ __ __ __ __ __ was Moses' successor as Israel's leader.

2. The Israelites were in the desert for ([I]YATRYROESF) __ __ __ __ __

   __ __ __ __ __

3. The Israelites built a (MN[R]OUTMEN) __ __ __ __ __ __ __ __ to

   remember God's help in crossing the River Jordan.

4. (GALILG[C]) __ __ __ __ __ __ means "circle of standing stones."

5. The Israelites marched around Jericho seven times on the

   (ETSVAY[O]DNEH) __ __ __ __ __ __ __ __ __ __.

6. The walls (ALELOPC[J]SD) __ __ __ __ __ __ __ __ __ __ when the

   priests blew their horns.

7. Joshua (EB[H]DYEO) __ __ __ __ __ __ God.

   Mystery Word ___ ___ ___ ___ ___ ___ ___

B. Fill in the Blanks

Fill in the blanks with the **key word(s)** to complete the statements below.

1. Only the priests blew the _____ _____.

2. God parted the waters of the _____ _____ on the way to Jericho.

3. The Israelites were divided into _____ _____.

4. The Ten Commandments were kept with the _____ ___ ____ _____.

C. True or False

Circle the letter in the first column before each statement that is true. Circle the letter in the second column before each statement that is false. The circled letters will reveal the mystery word.

<u>T</u>   <u>F</u>

L   O   1. God never let Moses see the Promised Land.

O   B   2. God supplied manna to the Israelites until they defeated Jericho.

E   R   3. Each of twelve tribes took a stone from the riverbed.

D   Y   4. The Israelites marched around Jericho 7 times each day.

This story teaches us that we need to trust and ___ ___ __ ___ God.

D. Essay Questions

What did God do to help the Israelites cross the Jordan River?

_____

_____

_____

What do you think was unusual about the defeat of the city of Jericho?

_____

_____

_____

God showed Joshua a simple solution to a problem that seemed impossible. Have you ever found a simple solution to a big problem? Explain.

_____

_____

_____

The Story of Samson
Judges: 13,14,15,16

After the death of Joshua, and the establishment of the twelve tribes in the land of Canaan, the Israelites often strayed from God. When they rebelled, He allowed **pagan** nations to oppress them. But, when they repented of their wickedness, the always-merciful God would raise up leaders among them called **judges** to deliver them from their enemies.

During the time when the Philistines dominated Israel, God raised up

Samson and blessed him with great **strength**. He was so strong that once he killed a lion with his bare hands! Samson's physical strength became a legend in the land.

However, Samson had many weaknesses. His greatest weakness was his love of the wrong women. He even violated Jewish Law, when he insisted on marrying a Philistine woman. But, God allowed this marriage to let Samson get close to his enemies. Samson soon learned that his new wife could not be trusted. In fact, her **betrayal** of him began a long period of fighting between Samson and the Philistines. The attacks and counter-attacks became so fierce that the Israelites feared for the safety of their families.

Finally, three thousand men of Israel came to **Samson** and pleaded with him to remember that they were under the rule of the Philistines. They told him that they had come to take him prisoner and to hand him over to the Philistines. But, just as the Philistines arrived, the Spirit of God came upon Samson. The two new ropes used to bind him melted away. Samson grabbed the jawbone of an ass lying nearby and attacked. He killed 1,000 Philistines that day.

For the next twenty years, Samson judged Israel. During this time, the Philistines never stopped looking for a way to bring him down. When he fell in love with another beautiful Philistine woman named **Delilah**, they finally saw their chance. A group of officers bribed Delilah

to get Samson to tell her the secret of his superhuman strength. Delilah's charm finally caused Samson, in a moment of human weakness, to reveal the secret of his strength. He told her that, in accordance with the Nazarite vow the angel of the Lord had revealed to his mother, if his head were **clean-shaven**, he would be no stronger than other men. So, while he slept, Delilah had Samson's head shaved. Then she called the spies who were waiting to capture him. The Philistines immediately gouged out his eyes and put him in bronze shackles. Tragically, the mighty Samson, blind and helpless, was forced to work in **humiliation** in the prison mill grinding corn.

Samson's **blindness** turned out to be a blessing. Only now could he see how he had failed God by wanting to be a part of the evil he had been sent to defeat. He finally learned that true power does not come from human strength but only from obeying the laws of God.

The Philistines saw their triumph over Samson as a victory of their pagan fish-god **Dagon** over the God of Israel. They held a grand celebration to further humiliate Samson and his God. They brought Samson to the center of the great hall in Gaza so they could **jeer** and make fun of him.

But God had mercy on Samson whose heart was changed. God had restored Samson's strength, as his hair grew longer. As he stood between the two **columns** that held up the roof of the temple, Samson cried out to God, "O Lord GOD, remember me! Strengthen me, O God, this last time that for my two eyes I may avenge myself once and for all on the Philistines." Then as he said, "Let me die with the Philistines," Samson pushed hard on the two columns and the whole temple collapsed killing him and more Philistines in one day than he had killed in his entire lifetime.

Name: _____ Date: _____

Key Words - The Story of Samson

betrayal	columns	humiliation	pagan
blindness	Dagon	jeer	Samson
clean-shaven	Delilah	judges	strength

A. Secret Code

Use the following code to find six **key words**. Then write the two given **key words** in code (7 and 8).

1. _____

2. _____

3. _____

4. _____

5. _____   7. _____
   S A M S O N

6. _____   8. _____
   D E L I A H

B. Matching

Match the **key words** on the left with the correct word or phrase on the right.

____ 1. Pagan	A. pagan fish-god
____ 2. Betrayal	B. deception
____ 3. Clean-shaven	C. injure self-respect
____ 4. Humiliation	D. all hair removed
____ 5. Blindness	E. make fun of
____ 6. Dagon	F. supports for a building
____ 7. Jeer	G. heathen
____ 8. Columns	H. inability to see

C. Scrambled Sentences

Unscramble the letters and words to form sentences. The scrambled words are not in the sentence order.

SWA   ~~FO~~   GJUDES   HATT   UP   ~~DGO~~
RDAISE   EON   ~~HET~~   MONSAS

_ _ _   O F   T H E   _ _   _ _ _ _   _ _ _ _   _

G O D   _ _ _ _ _ _   _ _   _ _ _ _   _ _ _ _ _ _   .

~~ASW~~   THSGENRT   SSEDBLE
MOSNSA   HTIW   RTEGA

_ _ _ _ _ _ _   W A S   _ _ _ _ _ _ _   _ _ _ _

_ _ _ _ _   _ _ _ _ _ _ _ _   .

ZAAG   NMSSOA   OT   OT   MIH
~~HTYE~~   ~~KOOT~~   EREJ   TA

T H E Y   T O O K   _ _ _ _ _ _   _ _   _ _ _ _

_ _   _ _ _ _ _   _ _   _ _ _ _   .

D. Essay Questions

Explain what happened to Samson after he failed God.

_____

_____

_____

_____

God blessed Samson with the gift of strength. What special talents or abilities has God blessed you with?

_____

_____

_____

_____

The Story of Ruth
Ruth 1, 2

Many years ago, in the time of Judges, **Bethlehem** suffered a severe drought. The crops had failed, and there was a great **famine** all around. Pressed by poverty, a true servant of God named Elimelech decided to take his wife, **Naomi** and their two sons, Mahlon and Chilon to the fertile plateaus of **Moab** across the Jordan River.

Soon the devout little family of four found their loyalty and devotion to God under a great strain. All of their neighbors neither loved nor served the true God but worshiped **idols** that were false gods they had created. Instead of taking part in the evils of Moab, Elimelech, Naomi, Mahlon and Chilon lived in such a way that their neighbors eventually came to respect them for their faith in God.

Then Elimelech suddenly died. His wife and sons were filled with grief. However, because they were too poor to return to Bethlehem, they buried Elimelech in the land of Moab. Within a few years Mahlon and Chilion married young women of Moab; one called Orpah, and the other, **Ruth**. Tragically, both of the young men Orpah and Ruth had just married died. Now there was only Naomi and her two daughters-in-law to comfort each other.

Even though the two young women were not of the same faith, Naomi

Ruth clings to Naomi

loved her **daughters-in-law** very much. In fact, Ruth and Orpah were so moved by Naomi's pious nature and upright conduct that they both gradually turned toward the Jewish faith.

News came to Naomi that the famine had ended in Israel and she told Ruth and Orpah of her desire to return home. She tenderly advised them to return to their parents because she thought it would be best for them.

Ruth and **Orpah** loved Naomi so deeply that they could not bear the thought of being separated from her. They begged Naomi either to stay with them in Moab, or else to let them go back with her to the land of Israel.

When she insisted on returning to her native land, they both journeyed with her to the border between Moab and Israel.

Orpah reconsidered the advice of her mother-in-law, said good-bye, and went back to live among her own people in Moab. But Ruth clung to Naomi, refused to leave her, and poured the depth of her love into these beautiful words: "Do not ask me to abandon or forsake you, for wherever you go I will go, wherever you lodge I will lodge, your people shall be my people, and your God my God. Wherever you die I will die, and there be buried. May the LORD do so and so to me, and more besides, if aught but death separates me from you!" Naomi graciously accepted this wonderful appeal, and the two women traveled together back to Bethlehem.

Ruth, in her genuine love for Naomi and for Naomi's God, had given up her nationality, the gods of her fathers, and the hope of marriage among her own people. By these **sacrifices** she proved her desire to become an Israelite in spirit and practice. With noble unselfishness she began a life of toil and self-denial in her new homeland, thinking only of the welfare and security of her beloved mother-in-law.

Naomi was given a hearty and gracious welcome by her relatives and friends. She was glad to be back among them, but in her heart-broken state over the loss of her husband and sons, she cried, "Do not call me Naomi (meaning pleasantness). Call me **Mara** (meaning bitter), for the Almighty has made it very bitter for me.

Naomi took Ruth into her home with love. She longed and prayed for the day that God might bless Ruth with a husband from the family of Elimelech. While gathering grain, Ruth met **Boaz**, another true servant of God. Through her marriage to him, God both answered Naomi's prayer and blessed Ruth by placing her in the **lineage** of Christ.

Ruth meets Boaz

Key Words - The Story of Ruth

Bethlehem	famine	Mara	Orpah
Boaz	idols	Moab	Ruth
daughters-in-law	lineage	Naomi	sacrifices

A. Naomi's Word Search

Fill in the blanks with the correct **key words** to complete the statements below. Then find and circle each of these **key word(s)** in the word search.

```
D A U G H T E R S I N L A W
F S A C R I F I C E S E G M
A R L U L I N E A G E X V O
I G X F H F O L I Z T N X I
E N A M A R A F O A N E O D
N N S O D E A W I O A R F O
I S A S R R L T E B O C M L
M L B O U O W D F S M A S S
A T A E M P I N B I R S B N
F F O M D I M O A B I A L L
M E H E L H T E B A D O N A
B I M H T U R H E T S L O X
```

Around _____ there was a great _____.
Elimelech took his wife _____ and his sons Mahlon and Chilon
and went to _____ where they could grow enough food for his
family. The people of this land worshipped _____, but
Elimelech and his family still held on to their faith in God. Soon after
Elimelech died, his sons married Orpah and _____. Then
the sons both tragically died.

The famine in Israel ended so Naomi decided to return home. She
told her _____ ___ _____ to return to their families. Ruth
refused to leave her mother-in-law. After they arrived in Bethlehem Naomi
told people to call her _____, meaning bitter. Ruth met and
married a man name _____. In doing so, she was placed in
the lineage of Jesus.

B. Hidden Word

Fill in the blanks with the **key words**. Then unscramble the letters with dots under them to determine the answer to statement #8.

1. things that are given up for someone else __ __ __ __ __ __ __ __ __

2. false gods __ __ __ __ __

3. food shortages __ __ __ __ __ __

4. Ruth & Orpah were Naomi's __ __ __ __ __ __ __ __ __ __ __ __ __ __ __ __

5. wife of Elimelech __ __ __ __ __

6. city where famine occurred __ __ __ __ __ __ __ __ __

7. Ruth's homeland __ __ __ __

8. This story explains how Ruth was placed in the __ __ __ __ __ __ __ of Jesus Christ.

C. Essay Questions

Why did Naomi and her family leave their home and why did she eventually choose to return home?

_____

_____

_____

What sacrifices did Ruth make in deciding to stay with Naomi?

_____

_____

_____

Like Naomi's family, what is something you do that shows those around you that you love God?

_____

_____

The Story of David and Goliath
1 Samuel 17

During the Israelites long journey of faith, God's answer to their prayers sometimes came in the form of a person. Most of the time (as in the case of Jesus) this was sometimes not exactly what the people expected or wanted. One example of this was when God sent David, a simple shepherd boy, to defeat the mighty Goliath, the champion warrior of the pagan and warlike **Philistines**.

Goliath was a giant from the city of Gath. HE WAS HUGE. **Goliath** towered over other men and weighed well over three hundred pounds. He wore a suit of heavy armor made of metal plates that overlapped like the scales on a fish. Goliath's head was protected with a brass helmet while heavy metal guards protected the lower part of his legs. He carried a sword that was five feet long that must have weighed twenty-five pounds.

On the other hand, David (who had been anointed by Samuel to one day become the King of Israel) was just a boy. He was the youngest son of Jesse of Bethlehem. From the beginning, David was full of **kindness** with a gentle and loving heart. As a boy, he did not use force to affect people. Instead, his gifts of music and later his beautiful writing inspired all those who would come to know him. It was David who wrote many beautiful **Psalms** we know and love today. Even Saul the King recognized these gifts in David at an early age. However, the only weapon David knew how to use was the sling he kept in his pocket to protect his father's sheep from the wolves in the fields. David became a very good shot with his sling and a stone.

One day, Jesse sent **David** to take food to his three brothers who were soldiers in the camp of King Saul. While there, David witnessed the showdown with the mighty Philistine army near Shochoh in the Land of Judah.

In those days, it often happened that when two opposing armies were in position for battle, but neither dared to attack, a **champion** from each side would meet in single combat. It was agreed that victory would belong to the army whose champion defeated his rival in the single combat.

David saw that Goliath was making just such a move. In fact, for the last forty-five days, he had been scornfully challenging the Israelites to send out a man in single battle against him. Goliath was making fun of both the **Israelites** and their God. David saw how all the Hebrew soldiers feared Goliath and would not stand up to him. Even Saul, the King, was frightened. But David was not afraid. His **confidence** and his faith in God convinced the king to allow him to do battle with the mighty Goliath. Saul and his entire army watched as this small **shepherd boy** approached the mighty giant. They were all amazed at his courage.

David turned down the king's offer for a suit of armor. He faced Goliath with only his staff, his sling and a stone. Goliath was insulted that the Israelites would send out a shepherd boy (such an unlikely **challenger**) to do battle with him. Goliath said to David, "Am I a dog that you come against me with a staff?" Even though David was small, his faith gave him great confidence. David said to Goliath, "I come against you in the name of the LORD of hosts." He then took one stone from his shepherd's bag, placed it in his **sling**, and hurled it with deadly aim at the forehead of the giant. The stone pierced the skull of the **giant**, and Goliath fell to the ground. David then rushed up to the fallen giant, drew Goliath's sword and cut off his head.

David grew strong in the sight of God and eventually became the King of Israel. We recall him each time we are reminded in stories about how Jesus was descended from the "House of David." In this story of David, we learn that strength is not just about physical size or abilities. When we love and follow God's commands, as in David's case, true strength is a gift from God that can be given to anyone regardless of age or size.

Key Words - The Story of David and Goliath

challenger	David	Israelites	Psalms
champion	giant	kindness	shepherd boy
confidence	Goliath	Philistines	sling

A. Crossword Puzzle

Fill in the blanks with the correct **key word(s)**.

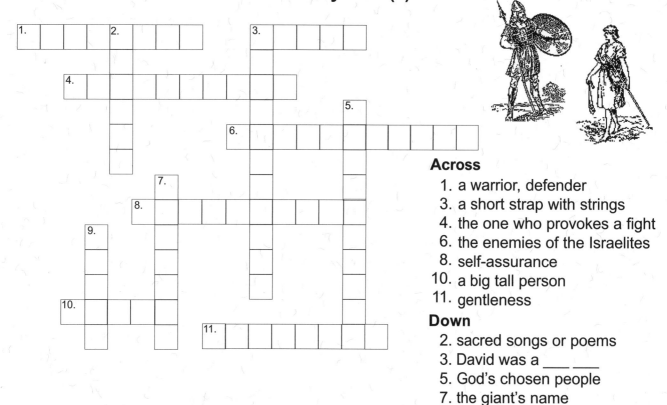

Across

1. a warrior, defender
3. a short strap with strings
4. the one who provokes a fight
6. the enemies of the Israelites
8. self-assurance
10. a big tall person
11. gentleness

Down

2. sacred songs or poems
3. David was a ___ ___
5. God's chosen people
7. the giant's name
9. Jesse's youngest son

B. True or False

Circle the letter in the first column before each statement that is true. Circle the letter in the second column before each statement that is false. The circled letters spell the mystery word.

True	False	
G	P	1. Goliath was an Israelite.
S	I	2. For 40 days the Philistines camped on a hill.
A	L	3. David was Jesse's youngest son.
N	L	4. David put on King Saul's armor.
M	T	5. Goliath was insulted to be challenged by a boy.
S	O	6. Jesus was a descendant of David.

Mystery word ___ ___ ___ ___ ___ ___

C. Scrambled Word Pairs

Each group of letters contains a name of a person from this story as well as a **key word**. Find and remove the letters of the person's name and the remaining letters reveal a **key word**. Write the answer in the blanks.

CHJEAMSSPIOEN

Removed name_____   Key word _____

DCHALLEVNIGERDA

Removed name _____   Key word _____

SACONFIUDENCLEME

Removed name _____   Key word _____

KINGODNELIASTHS

Removed name _____   Key word _____

D. Essay Questions

How did Goliath react to David's challenge?

_____

_____

_____

Why did David use his sling instead of King Saul's armor and sword?

_____

_____

_____

Even though David was small he was able to defeat Goliath with God's help. Is there something that you are or were afraid to do because you were worried about your size or your age? Explain.

_____

_____

The Story of David the King of Israel

2 Samuel 2

David being anointed by Samuel

In the history of Israel, no King was more beloved by God than His good and faithful servant, **David**. In a wonderful example of God's love and forgiveness, David, despite his human weaknesses, was to become the greatest king Israel had ever known.

God's favor was first bestowed on David through the anointing by the prophet **Samuel.** He was just a shepherd boy! Soon after this time, David's triumph over the evil Philistine giant, Goliath was even more proof that David was truly chosen by God.

David was known to have many talents and a gentle and playful spirit. Even King Saul recognized these talents when he brought David into his service as a musician in his court. Saul often called on David to play his harp to comfort him when he was in a bad mood. Because Saul recognized that God was with

David, he later made him a general in his army to continue the fight against the enemies of Israel. God's blessing continued to be with David as a military leader. He was loved by the soldiers under his command and respected by his enemies.

David plays music for Saul

It didn't take long for Saul to recognize that David was blessed by God. He became very jealous of David's successes and popularity. Several times, Saul even plotted to kill David. However, God would always protect David and allow him to escape from any danger. Even though he feared Saul when the King was alive, David mourned him and especially his son **Jonathan** (who was David's friend) when they were killed by the Philistines. David even chanted an **elegy** (a poem of lament and praise for the dead) for Saul and Jonathan upon learning of their deaths.

After serving as the King of **Judah** for seven years, the other tribes of Israel came to David and anointed him King over all of Israel. They reminded him that even when Saul was their king, it was David that they trusted in battle and respected as a leader. Many of the Israelites did not realize that in calling for David to be their king, they were in fact following the will of God. Few if any of them remembered that David was the shepherd boy who had been anointed by the prophet Samuel through the will of God.

David was **thirty** years old when he became King and he reigned for forty years. One of David's most important accomplishments as king was the capture of the well-fortified city of **Jerusalem**. He was the first King to make Jerusalem the capital of Israel. From this day forward, Jerusalem has been known as the "**City of David**." David is also responsible for moving the Ark of the Covenant (the chest containing the manna and the Ten Commandments) to Jerusalem. With God's blessing, through the prophet Nathan, David also began the plans to construct a temple that would be a suitable place of honor for the Ark of the Covenant.

But even David was not always faithful to God. In his weakness, his eye was taken by a beautiful woman named **Bathsheba** who was the wife of one of his soldiers. Rather than turning away from this temptation, David arranged to have Uriah, her husband, moved to the most dangerous spot of the battle so that he might be killed. After Uriah was killed, David took Bathsheba as his wife. God was not pleased with the sin David had committed. God sent the prophet Nathan to David to make him see the evil that he had done. When David saw how seriously he had sinned through a **parable** (a short story containing a moral lesson) that Nathan told him, he repented his sin and begged God's forgiveness.

As a punishment for his sin, David and Bathsheba's child was stricken with a serious illness. For several days David fasted and prayed to God that his child might be spared but the child died. In His infinite **mercy**, God forgave David for his sin and restored His blessings upon him. God even gave David a second child by his wife Bathsheba - a son named Solomon (a name which means **Beloved of God**) who was destined to be the next King of Israel.

Key Words - The Story of David the King of Israel

Bathsheba	David	Jonathan	parable
Beloved of God	elegy	Judah	Samuel
City of David	Jerusalem	mercy	thirty

A. Mystery Person Matching

Match the key words on the left with the correct phrase on the right.
Then unscramble the letters to identify the mystery person.

M. Bathsheba   _____ 1. David's close friend

A. elegy   _____ 2. Nathan confronted David with his sin using this

U. parable   _____ 3. Solomon's name means this

S. Jonathan   _____ 4. David had her husband killed in battle

E. mercy   _____ 5. God had _____ on David and forgave him.

L. Beloved of God   _____ 6. A poem of lament and praise for the dead

Mystery Person ___ ___ ___ ___ ___ ___

B. Number Magic Code

Use the code in the box to reveal the missing **key word(s)**.

	1	2	3	4	5	6
1	A	B	C	D	E	F
2	G	H	I	J	K	L
3	M	N	O	P	Q	R
4	S	T	U	V	W	X
5	Y	Z				

A total of 7 could be represented
by these letters F, K, P, U or Z

Example: P = 4 + 3 = 7

1. __ __ __ __ __, was __ __ __ __ __ __ years old, when he became King of
    5 2 8 5 5   6 4 5 9 6 6

__ __ __ __ __ .
6 7 5 2 4

2. During his reign he captured __ __ __ __ __ __ __ __ and made it his
                          6 6 9 7 5 2 8 6 4

capital. From then on it was called the __ __ __ __ __ __ __ __ __ __ __ .
                                       4 5 6 6 6 7   5 2 8 5 5

C. True or False

Put the letter T on the line in front of each statement that is true. Put the letter F in the line in front of each statement that is false.

_____ 1. A parable is a story that teaches a lesson.

_____ 2. David was happy when the Philistines killed Saul.

_____ 3. Saul's son Jonathan was David's close friend.

_____ 4. Samuel anointed David as King when he was a boy.

_____ 5. Solomon was David's firstborn by Bathsheba.

_____ 6. God never forgave David for his sins.

D. Essay Questions

Even though King Saul appointed David to his court, he still wanted to kill him. Why?

_____

_____

_____

_____

David's story teaches us that even the least likely person in our eyes can become someone great in God's eyes. What do you think God has planned for you?

_____

_____

_____

_____

The Story of Solomon
1 Kings 1:29 - 3:28

Before he died, **David**, the **King of Israel**, proclaimed that **Solomon**, his son, should **succeed** (or follow) him as King. It was Solomon who built the magnificent palace and the great temple in Jerusalem as well as the wall around the city. Solomon loved the Lord and obeyed the statutes of his father David. God rewarded him by making him the wisest of all kings. All people throughout Israel and Egypt learned of his **reputation** for great knowledge and inspired wisdom.

But these gifts did not just happen. God granted them to Solomon because he asked for them at a place called **Gibeon**. It happened one night (after he had offered sacrifices to God) when the Lord appeared to Solomon in a **dream**. God said to him, "Ask something of me and I will give it to you." Solomon was

very humble before God. He praised God and thanked Him for the blessings on his father David, upon the people of Israel and upon himself. Then, the young king asked God only for "an understanding heart to judge Your people and to **distinguish right from wrong**." Even though he could have asked for anything in the world, Solomon was not selfish when he made his request. He did not ask for a long life for himself or for riches or even for the punishment of his enemies. Instead, Solomon asked God to give him the wisdom to always know the difference between right and wrong.

God was very pleased that Solomon had made this request. He told Solomon that He would give him a heart more wise and understanding than anyone who had ever lived in the past or anyone who would ever live in the future. In addition, because he was so humble, God promised Solomon that He would also grant him great riches and make him famous throughout the land. God also promised Solomon that he would live a long life. When Solomon awoke from this dream, he went to the temple and prayed.

Solomon's **wisdom** was soon put to the test. One day, two women came to him with a very serious problem. Each of the women (who lived together) had recently given birth to a baby boy but one of the babies had died. The first woman who spoke to Solomon told him that the other woman's baby had died during the night and that she had switched her dead baby for the first woman's live  baby. When the first woman woke up, she was holding the dead baby by her side. She told Solomon that she knew that this baby was not hers. She said that the live baby was hers. The other woman told exactly the opposite story. She denied that she had **switched** the babies. The two women got into a big argument right in front of the King. Solomon realized that he had to make a difficult decision.

Solomon thought for a moment. Then he commanded his servant to bring his sword. Solomon said, "Cut the living child in two, and give half to one woman and half to the other." Immediately, the first woman who was the actual mother of the child cried out to Solomon, "Please, my lord, give her the living child - please do not kill it!" Solomon knew that only the real mother would love her baby so much that she would rather give him up than to see him killed. Then, showing the wisdom God had given him, Solomon said, "Give the first one the living child . . . for she is the mother."

Solomon's reputation for wisdom quickly spread throughout the land and the known world. He built a magnificnet temple in Jerusalem that was superior to anything ever built at that time. He enjoyed a long life and was blessed with many riches. The story of Solomon teaches us to remain **humble** before God in both our actions and prayers. In doing so, we find that our **reward** is often greater and more valuable than anything we could ever have wished for in the first place.

Key Words - The Story of Solomon

David	Gibeon	reputation	succeed
distinguish right from wrong	humble	reward	switched
dream	King of Israel	Solomon	wisdom

A. Letter Addition

Find the missing letters that add up to the number below the blanks. The completed blanks will reveal some **key words**. One letter is done for you.

	1	2	3	4
1	S	A	L	D
2	A	O	O	V
3	O	M	N	E
4	I	D	G	B

Statement 1

Example: 3 + 1 = 4

4 = A, L, or O

	5	6	7	8
5	E	L	T	I
6	O	D	M	S
7	H	S	W	D
8	C	W	N	O

Statement 2

1. S __ __ __ __ __ __ was the son of __ __ __ __ and it was at
      2 4 4 5 5 4 6   5 3 6 5 6

    __ __ __ __ __ __ that he asked God for the gifts of knowledge and
     7 5 8 7 4 6

    inspired wisdom.

2. __ __ __ __ __ __ __'S __ __ __ __ __ __ was tested by a woman
    13 11 11 16 13 11 15   14 13 14 12 16 13

    who claimed that another woman had __ __ __ __ __ __ __ __ babies
                                       13 14 13 12 13 12 10 15

    with hers.

B. Matching

Match the **key words** on the left with the correct phrase on the right.

_____ 1. Succeed   A. an image during sleep

_____ 2. Reputation   B. to exchange one for another

_____ 3. Reward   C. to follow or come after

_____ 4. Humble   D. not proud or haughty

_____ 5. Switched   E. your history according to others

_____ 6. Dream   F. a prize awarded for doing good

C. Missing Consonants

Use the consonants in the box to complete the **key words** in the sentences below.
Hint: Cross them off as you go.

```
B  M  D  M  T  R  W  H  N
M  L  F  T  W  N  D  R  R
D  R  R  R  F  G  G  K  T
L  P  C  G  R  S  D  S  N
T  R  H  S  C  H  S  N  G
```

1. Solomon was to __u__ __ ee __ his father David as the

   __ i __ __ o __   l __ __ ae__.

2. Solomon's __e __ u__ a__io__ became well known in Israel and Egypt.

3. In a __ __ea__ Solomon asked for the wisdom to __ i __ __ i __ __ui __ __

   __ i __ __ __   __ __o __   __ __ o __ __.

4. Solomon teaches us that if we remain __ u __ __ __e before God, our

   __ e__ a __ __ will be greater than we could ever wish for.

D. Essay Questions

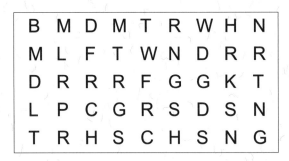

How did Solomon determine who the real mother of the baby was?

_____

_____

_____

_____

What would you request from God if He said "Ask something of Me and I
will give it to you?" Explain.

_____

_____

_____

_____

The Story of Jonah
Book of Jonah

Jonah was a prophet in the Northern Kingdom of Israel during the reign of Jeroboam II. One day, the Lord called Jonah to go on a mission to **Nineveh**, the capital of the great Assyrian Empire. This was a dangerous mission. Everyone knew that the Assyrians were a very violent and wicked people. For centuries, Assyrian kings had fought against all the nations around them carrying off their possessions and making slaves of their people. Jonah and his people feared **Assyria**.

God told Jonah to announce to Nineveh that God would destroy the city in forty days unless the people **repented** (turned away from their wickedness). Jonah could not believe it. He did not want God to give Nineveh a chance to escape destruction. So, rather than doing as God had told him, Jonah decided to run away. He went to Joppa and boarded a ship to **Tarshish** a town at the western end of the Mediterranean Sea.

God hurled a great wind upon the sea. The boat Jonah was on was tossed in the waves until it was at the point of breaking up. The sailors were frightened and cried out to their individual gods. They even threw the cargo overboard hoping to lighten the ship. Nothing helped! The captain found Jonah sleeping in the **hold** (bottom) of the ship and said to him, "What are you doing asleep? Rise up, call upon your God! Perhaps God will be mindful of us so that we may not perish."

Jonah told the sailors that he was a **Hebrew** and worshiped "the God of heaven, who made the sea and the dry land." Now the sailors were even more

afraid. Jonah told them "Pick me up and throw me into the sea, that it may quiet down for you; since I know it is because of me that this violent storm has come upon you." The men were afraid that God would punish them for murdering His **prophet** so they tried rowing for the shore, but the storm grew even worse. Finally, they cried out to the Lord, "We beseech you, O LORD, let us not perish for taking this man's life . . " They asked God not to punish them for what they were about to do. Then they threw Jonah into the sea. At that moment, the storm ended. The grateful sailors worshiped God offering sacrifices and making vows to Him.

Instead of drowning, Jonah was swallowed by a **great fish**. God kept him completely safe in the belly of the fish for **three days**. Jonah prayed for forgiveness for his sin and promised to obey God in the future if he were rescued. God caused the fish to spit Jonah out on the shores of his homeland and Jonah sang a song of praise to God for saving him.

God again sent Jonah to preach to Nineveh. This time Jonah promptly obeyed. He gave the people God's message. The entire city put on **sackcloth** and ashes to show their repentant hearts. The king even issued a decree that everyone must ask God's forgiveness and **fast** (not to eat or drink anything). When God saw these actions, He decided not to punish Nineveh.

Jonah again became angry that any people other than the Hebrews could find favor with God. He told God that this was exactly what he was afraid was going to happen. In his **jealousy**, he even wished to die rather than to have to live to see God's mercy extended to others. God said to him, "Have you reason to be angry?"

The story of Jonah teaches us that there have always been people who thought they should have God's blessings all to themselves. However, what we see in this story is an example of God's love for all people, even those who may have turned away from Him. This story challenges us to do more than accept God's love and forgiveness for ourselves. We should also rejoice when we see others accept it - - even people we don't like.

Key Words - The Story of Jonah

Assyria	Hebrew	Nineveh	sackcloth
fast	hold	prophet	Tarshish
great fish	jealousy	repented	three days

A. Missing Letters

Fill in the blanks with the letters from the box below. Shade all the letters you have used in the box. Then use the <u>unshaded</u> letters to reveal the answer to the mystery words.

1. __ i n e __ e __

2. __ s __ y __ i a

3. __ __ r __ h i s __

4. r __ __ e n t e __

5. __ e __ r e __

6. h __ l __

7. j e __ __ o u __ y

8. __ a __ k __ __ o t __

9. __ a __ t

10. p __ o __ __ e t

A	B	H	S	F	R	R	D
O	W	F	S	S	C	S	H
S	I	H	V	L	E	P	G
H	A	A	L	R	D	C	H
T	N	T	H	A	E	P	S

Mystery Words:

God kept Jonah safe in the belly of a ___ ___ ___ ___ ___   ___ ___ ___ ___.

B. True or False

Put the letter T on the line in front of each statement that is true. Put the letter F in the line in front of each statement that is false.

_____ 1. Jonah and his people feared the Assyrians.

_____ 2. The sailors threw Jonah overboard when they knew who he was.

_____ 3. Jonah was in the belly of the great fish for three days.

_____ 4. The people of Nineveh refused to listen to Jonah and turn from sin.

_____ 5. Jonah was jealous of God offering mercy to the wicked Assyrians.

C. Matching

Match the key word on the left with the correct phrase on the right.

_____ 1. Jealousy   A. the clothes worn to show repentance

_____ 2. Nineveh   B. the country where Nineveh was located

_____ 3. Assyria   C. Jonah's feeling toward the Assyrians

_____ 4. Tarshish   D. to go without food or water

_____ 5. Sackcloth   E. the bottom of a boat where Jonah slept

_____ 6. Fast   F. Jonah was fleeing to this city.

_____ 7. Hold   G. the city where God sent Jonah

_____ 8. Repented   H. turned away from sin/wickedness

D. Essay Questions

Why didn't Jonah want to go to Nineveh? Why didn't he like God offering mercy to the people of Nineveh who were known for their wickedness?

_____

_____

_____

The story teaches us that we should rejoice in knowing that God still loves us even if we don't deserve it. Has there ever been a time when you felt like you didn't deserve God's love?

_____

_____

_____

The Story of Daniel in the Lions' Den
Daniel 6

When **Media** and Persia were merged to become **Babylon**, Darius the Great, a Mede, became the king. He named Daniel as one of three regional supervisors in his kingdom even though Daniel was an Israelite. The supervisor's job was to oversee the 120 **satraps** or Persian Governors the king had appointed and to safeguard his interests throughout the land. Daniel performed these duties very well. Through God's grace and with a strong faith he did much better than the other supervisors and all the **governors**. In fact, the king was so pleased that he was even considering giving Daniel authority over his entire kingdom.

When the other two supervisors and the governors learned that the king might further honor Daniel by giving him one of the highest ranks of authority, their hearts were filled with jealousy and rage. In **anger**, the supervisors and governors began to plot Daniel's downfall. They knew Daniel's character and official conduct were without fault so they decided to use his faith in God as an excuse to get rid of him.

Daniel's enemies designed an evil plot. They came to the king in large numbers saying to him, "King Darius, live forever!" Then after diverting his attention, they tricked him into signing a decree that no man in the kingdom should be permitted to offer any prayer to any God or any petition to any man for thirty days except to the king. Anyone who broke the law would be immediately thrown into the lions' den, a fate that would lead to certain death. The evil men reminded Darius that, as king, anything he signed under Mede and Persian law could not be changed and could not be taken back. King

Darius signed the paper making this new decree the law of the land.

Daniel had always prayed three times a day and could not betray God regardless of the risk to his own life. Knowing this, the evil men were certain that this decree would entrap Daniel. They hid outside his house to catch him. When they saw that **Daniel** was kneeling in prayer before an open window facing toward Jerusalem, they rushed to tell the king.

The evil men asked the **king** if he remembered the unchangeable law. The king told them that he did remember the law. Then they reported that Daniel was breaking the new law by continuing to pray to God each day. They demanded that Darius follow the letter of the new law and punish Daniel by throwing him into the lions' den.

Darius was greatly upset and troubled; not with Daniel, but with himself for being tricked into issuing a decree which threatened the life of his most trusted official. He spent the whole day trying to find some way to avoid casting Daniel into the lions' den, but under the rigid law there was no way out. As Daniel was thrown into the den of hungry, ferocious lions the king said, "May your God, whom you serve so constantly save you." With that, a stone was placed over the mouth of the cave.

After a long, sleepless night in which the king was tortured by thoughts of the injustice done to Daniel, Darius rushed to the **lions' den**. As he drew near he called out to Daniel in a sorrowful voice, "O Daniel, servant of the living God, has the God whom you serve so constantly been able to save you from the lions?" A cheerful voice answered, "O king, live forever!" Daniel assured the king that God had sent an **angel** and closed the lions' mouths so that they had done him no harm. Daniel was unhurt because he placed his total **trust** in God.

The king was very happy that Daniel was not hurt and ordered that he be removed from the lions' den. Instead, those who plotted Daniel's death were thrown into the lions' den as a just punishment.

Upon seeing the power of Daniel's faith and how God had delivered him from the lions' den, King Darius wrote a new **decree** to the nations and people of every language. It began, "All peace to you! I decree that throughout my royal domain the God of Daniel is to be reverenced and feared . . ."

Daniel lived and prospered even after the death of King Darius.

Key Words - The Story of Daniel in the Lions' Den

angel	Daniel	governor	Media
anger	Darius	king	satrap
Babylon	decree	lions' den	trust

A. Crossword Puzzle

Complete the following crossword puzzle using the **key words**.

ACROSS

3. the _____ Den
4. God's Servant
5. Daniel was saved by his _____ in God.
6. _____ & Persia
9. the evil men also felt this toward Daniel
10. Darius' Kingdom
11. King _____
12. there were 120 of these Persian _____

DOWN

1. a Persian Governor
2. a written law issued
7. God sent him to protect Daniel in the lions' den.
8. not Media but _____

B. Matching

Match the **key word** on the left with the correct phrase on the right.

_____ Babylon   A. God sent him to close the lions' mouths.

_____ Daniel   B. the Persian word for governor

_____ Media   C. a formal order issued in writing by the King

_____ Satrap   D. the King of Babylon

_____ Trust   E. His trust in God saved him from certain death.

_____ Darius   F. the name given to the kingdom that was created after Media and Persia were united

_____ Den   G. to have total faith

_____ Angel   H. a place where lions are kept

_____ Decree   I. merged with Persia to become Babylon

C. Essay Questions

Why did the evil supervisors and governors plot against Daniel?

_____

_____

_____

Have you ever felt God's protection in a time of danger? Explain.

_____

_____

_____

The Story of the Annunciation & Birth of Jesus
Luke 1, 2

Six months after Elizabeth and Zacharias learned of the coming birth of their son (who was John the Baptist), the angel **Gabriel** also appeared to Mary of Nazareth. Mary was betrothed (promised) to a carpenter named Joseph who was a member of the house of David. Mary and Joseph both had a very strong faith. They lived simple lives in humble obedience of the laws of God.

The angel said to **Mary**, "Hail, favored one! The Lord is with you." Mary was overcome with emotion. The angel comforted her by saying, "Do not be afraid, Mary, for your have found favor with God. Behold, you will conceive in

your womb and bear a son, and you shall name Him **Jesus**. He will be great and will be called **Son of the Most High,** and the Lord God will give Him the throne of David his father, and He will rule over the house of Jacob forever, and of His kingdom there will be no end."

Mary asked the angel how this could be since she was not yet married. The angel answered, "The Holy Spirit will come upon you, and the power of the most high will overshadow you.

Therefore the child to be born will be called holy, the Son of God." The angel informed Mary that her cousin **Elizabeth** was also going to have a baby. Mary was very happy. Before the angel left, she accepted God's message, by saying, "Behold, I am the handmaid of the Lord. May it be done to me according to your word."

Soon, Mary went to the hill country to share the wonderful news with her cousin Elizabeth. When Mary entered the house Elizabeth greeted her by saying, "Most blessed are you among women, and blessed is the fruit of your womb." Mary responded to Elizabeth with a beautiful prayer called the **Magnificat**. It begins, "My soul proclaims the greatness of the Lord; my spirit rejoices in God my savior." Mary stayed with Elizabeth for three months before returning home to Nazareth.

Shortly before Jesus was born, the Roman Emperor Caesar Augustus issued a **decree** (an order issued by one in authority) that everyone who lived under his rule must register to be counted. In keeping with customs, all Jewish people traveled to the hometown of their **ancestors** to be counted. Since Mary and Joseph were both of the House of David, this meant that they must return to the small town of **Bethlehem** in Judea which was a long eighty-mile journey from Nazareth in Galilee.

The journey was especially long and hard for Mary who was expecting a child any day. To make things worse, when they arrived in Bethlehem, there was no place for them to stay. All the houses and hotels were already filled with the hundreds of other people that had also come for the **census**. The only place they could find to be warm was in a **stable**, a place where cattle were fed. It was there that the baby Jesus was born!

In the countryside there were some **shepherds** watching their sheep. Suddenly, an angel appeared to them which freightened them. The angel said to them, "Do not be afraid; for behold, I proclaim to you good news of great joy that will be for all the people." He went on, "For today in the city of David a savior has been born for you who is Messiah and Lord." Then the sky was filled with angels and heavenly hosts praising God and saying "Glory to God in the highest and on earth peace to those on whom His favor rests."

The shepherds hurried into Bethlehem and found the stable where Jesus was born. There, they worshipped Him with humble hearts. They returned to their fields praising and glorifying God for all that they had heard and seen. Mary kept these wonderful things to herself as she took her new son home and raised him with love as a true servant of God.

Name: _____ Date: _____

Key Words - The Story of the Annunciation & Birth of Jesus

ancestors	census	Gabriel	shepherds
Bethlehem	decree	Magnificat	stable
betrothed	Elizabeth	Mary	Son of the Most High

A. Crossword

Fill in the squares with the **key words** that answer the clues below.

T
H
E
M
A
G
N
I
F
I
C
A
T

1. a place where cattle are fed and housed
2. They watch sheep.
3. our past relatives
4. a small town in Galilee
5. He announced the births of both John the Baptist and Jesus.
6. another name for Jesus
7. the counting of people
8. Mary's cousin
9. an order issued by one in authority
10. the mother of Jesus
11. promised in marriage

B. Fill in the Star

Put the answer to the clues below over the appropriate spot in the star.

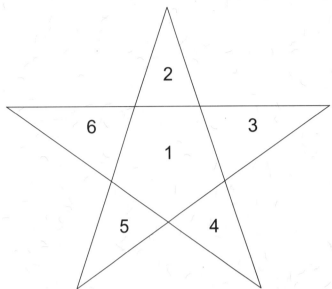

1. He was called **Son of the Most High**
2. the mother of Jesus
3. John's mother and Mary's cousin
4. they came to worship the baby
5. he appeared to Mary
6. the city where the census was taken

C. Essay Questions

What is the Magnificat?

_____

_____

_____

_____

Why do you think Jesus was born in such simple surroundings?

_____

_____

_____

_____

The Story of the Presentation of Jesus
Luke 2:22-38

Soon after the birth of Jesus, Mary and Joseph moved into a humble dwelling place where they made their first home for a short period of time. Mary and Joseph were very faithful to **Jewish** law. As new parents, this law called for them to take Jesus to the temple and present Him to God with offerings of sacrifice and praise. They did this at the temple in Jerusalem forty days after Jesus was born.

The Presentation of the baby Jesus to God in the temple took place only after the period of purification for Mary. According to Mosaic law (the law according to the teachings of Moses), the woman who gave birth to a boy was unable for forty days to touch anything sacred or to enter the temple. When this period was over, she was required to offer a one year-old lamb as a burnt offering and a **turtledove** or a young pigeon as a peace offering for the **atonement** of sin in the world. If the woman could not afford a lamb she could offer two turtledoves or two pigeons. This is what Mary did that day.

There was an old man named **Simeon** in the temple the day Mary and Joseph took Jesus there. Simeon was a good and humble man of great faith. God had assured him, through the Holy Spirit, that he would not die until he had seen the promised **Messiah**. As

Mary and Joseph were presenting Jesus before the altar of God, Simeon was moved by the **Holy Spirit**. He knew in his heart that Jesus was the Messiah he had been waiting to see. Taking the child into his arms and speaking with deep emotion, the faithful old man said, "Now, Master, You may let Your servant go in peace. According to Your word, for my eyes have seen Your salvation, which You prepared in sight of all the peoples, a light for revelation to the Geniles, and glory for Your people Israel."

Simeon's words were a reminder to Mary and Joseph that the birth of Jesus was the **fulfillment** of prophecy in the Old Testament. The angel Gabriel had already told them that Jesus was the Son of God. But, they were still amazed that Simeon, a total stranger to them, recognized Jesus as the Savior God had promised to send. Simeon then blessed the Holy Family and said to Mary, "Behold, this child is destined for the fall and rise of many in Israel, and to be a sign that will be contradicted, and you yourself a sword will pierce so that the thoughts of many hearts may be revealed."

Also in the temple that day was a very old woman, a true servant of God named **Anna**. She was eighty-four years old, a prophetess, and the daughter of Phanuel of the tribe of Asher. She had been a widow for many years and spent all of her time fasting and praying in the temple. In fact, she was so committed to God, that she never left the **temple,** day or night.

Anna came forward just as Simeon finished speaking to Mary. She gave thanks to God and told all the people who were gathered there about the work of redemption that this infant Jesus would accomplish as an adult in **Jerusalem**.

Mary and Joseph did not know at the time exactly what Simeon and Anna meant by what they said. How could they know how true Simeon's words would be? A **sword of sorrow** at the suffering and death of Jesus would indeed pierce Mary's heart only thirty-three years later. How could they know how Jesus was to redeem all of the world as Anna had said? What Mary and Joseph did know was that God had given them a very special child – His Son. After the **Presentation**, Jesus grew in the love and care of Mary and Joseph.

Name: _____ Date: _____

Key Words - The Story of the Presentation of Jesus

Anna	Holy Spirit	Messiah	sword of sorrow
atonement	Jerusalem	presentation	temple
fulfillment	Jewish	Simeon	turtledove

A. Fill in the Blanks

Fill in the blanks below with the letters of the alphabet as follows: A = 1, B = 2, C = 3 etc. Each of the answers is from the list of **key words**. Then solve the puzzle at the bottom of the page using only the circled letters.

1. The __ __ __ __ Ⓞ __ __ __ __ __ moved Simeon to recognize Jesus.
   8 15 12 25   19 16 9 18 9 20

2. Mary and Joseph were very faithful to __ __ __ Ⓞ __ __ laws and tradition.
   10 5 23 9 19 8

3. The temple was in the city of __ __ __ __ __ __ __ __ Ⓞ.
   10 5 18 21 19 1 12 5 13

4. Mary and Joseph took Jesus to the __ Ⓞ __ __ __ __ for the Presentation.
   20 5 13 16 12 5

5. Mary offered a young pigeon as __ __ Ⓞ __ __ __ __ Ⓞ __ for the sins
   of the world.   1 20 15 14 5 13 5 14 20

6. Ⓞ Ⓞ __ __ was eighty-four years old before she met Jesus as an infant.
   1 14 14 1

7. God had promised __ __ __ __ __ Ⓞ that he would live to see
   Jesus the Savior. 19 9 13 5 15 14

8. All of those who heard Simeon and Anna in the temple on the day of Jesus'
   Presentation heard them tell that Jesus was the __ __ __ __ __ Ⓞ __.
   13 5 19 19 9 1 8

Puzzle: They were there: ___ ___ ___ ___ ___ ___ & ___ ___ ___ ___

B. Multiple Choice

Choose the letter of the **key word(s)** that best complete the sentences.

_____ 1. Simeon told Mary that her heart would one day be pierced with a

      a. Mosaic law   b. sword of sorrow   c. prophecy   d. servant

_____ 2. Mary's sacrifice for sin in the world

      a. Jerusalem   b. purification   c. atonement   d. fulfillment

_____ 3. Anna was a

      a. servant of God   b. prophetess   c. widow   d. all of these

_____ 4. Mary offered a pigeon and a dove in sacrifice as an atonement for

      a. sin in the world   b. Jerusalem   c. the Holy Spirit   d. Simeon

_____ 5. Simeon knew that Jesus was

      a. the Messiah   b. God's Son   c. a fulfillment   d. all of these

_____ 6. In Mosaic Law, the length of the purification time after the birth of a son

      a. in Jerusalem   b. on holy days   c. forty days   d. ever

C. Essay Question

What "sword of sorrow" would later pierce Mary's heart?

_____

_____

_____

The Story of the Finding in the Temple
Luke 2: 41-52

With the death of Herod, the immediate threat against Jesus' life ended. The angel of the Lord appeared to **Joseph** and told him that it was safe to return home. So Joseph, Mary and Jesus journeyed to their home in **Nazareth**, a small town in Galilee.

The Bible tells us that Jesus "grew and became strong, filled with wisdom and the favor of God." We are not told about the details of His life as a boy. However we do know some information based on what is related to us in other parts of the Bible. We know Jesus is spoken of as both a **carpenter** and a carpenter's son. It appears that He assisted Joseph in his chosen trade. Jesus probably grew up as did other Jewish boys of that age, taking part in the youthful sports of the day, mingling with neighbors and attending the social and religious activities of the community.

Because Joseph and **Mary** were not wealthy in material things, Jesus was probably brought up in a very simple home. His house may have been made of walls of whitewashed stones and its floors may have been bare earth. The furniture might have consisted of a small table or two, a wooden chest for clothing, woven baskets for food, earthen jars for water, and a stand from which a stone lamp gave out a flickering light. The beds in that time were often made of woven rugs, which were kept on a platform at one end of the room during the day and spread on the earthen floor at night. Unlike many children today, Jesus grew up with very few material things.

We know that Jesus grew up in a very loving home. As a boy, Jesus showed His love for both Mary and Joseph as well as His love for God. He learned and lived the **scriptures** each and every day. Jesus may have even been sent to school in the village **synagogue**, where He was taught to read. Children of this time were instructed in the word of God from scrolls containing the books of the Old Testament, and required to memorize long passages from the Law, the Prophets, and the Psalms.

When Jesus was a boy of twelve, the **age of reason** in the Jewish tradition, He was allowed to accompany Mary and Joseph to Jerusalem for the annual feast of the **Passover**. This was the feast which reminded the Jewish people of the time when the angel of death stalked the land of Egypt, taking the firstborn in every home which was not protected by the blood of a lamb sprinkled on the doorposts.

Jesus probably walked among the courts of the temple, and looked upon the great altar with its burning sacrifices. He may have watched the priests in their white robes as they ministered about the altar, and heard the **Rabbis** explain the laws of Israel while on this trip. In fact, He may have been so completely fascinated with these sacred proceedings that He did not realize that His parents and friends had started on the journey back to Nazareth.

There was a large **caravan** of pilgrims traveling the road which Mary and Joseph took on their way home. They went for a whole day before they realized Jesus was missing. Mary and Joseph returned to **Jerusalem** at once to search for Him. It took three days to find Him. His parents found Him conversing with the learned teachers in the temple and astonishing them with His wisdom. Mary gently **reprimanded** Jesus for staying behind, and He replied, "Why were you looking for Me? Did you not know that I must be in My Father's house?" At the time, neither Joseph nor Mary fully understood what Jesus meant.

Thanking God that they had found Him, Mary and Joseph took Jesus and returned to Nazareth. Jesus grew in wisdom and the favor of God.

Name: _____ Date: _____

Key Words - The Story of the Finding in the Temple

age of reason	Jerusalem	Nazareth	reprimanded
caravan	Joseph	Passover	scriptures
carpenter	Mary	Rabbis	synagogue

A. Letters in a Box

Five **key words** are scrambled in the boxes below. Unscramble each word and write it in the space under the box. Use the clues under the spaces to help you reveal the answer.

O	■	H	■
E	S	J	P

A	V	R	■
A	C	A	N

A	■	R
■	M	Y

_____   _____   _____
Jesus' father   People traveling together   Jesus' mother

C	R	R	T	P	■
U	■	S	I	E	S

E	R	P	A	N
E	■	C	T	R

_____   _____
Word of God   Joseph's occupation

B. Fill in the Blanks

Fill in the blanks with correct **key word(s)**.

1. In the Jewish tradition, when a boy was twelve years old he was said to be at the _____.

2. Jesus and his family traveled with many other people in a large _____ to Jerusalem and back home again.

3. Jesus may have been taught to read at the village _____.

4. Jesus listened to the _____ explain the laws of Israel.

5. Jesus worked with his father as a _____.

C. Matching

Match the **key word** on the left with the correct phrase on the right.

_____ Reprimand	A. the town in Galilee where Jesus grew up
_____ Synagogue	B. the town where Mary, Joseph and Jesus traveled to celebrate Passover
_____ Jerusalem	C. learned teachers
_____ Passover	D. a temple
_____ Rabbis	E. a feast that reminded the Jewish people of their history
_____ Nazareth	F. to gently discipline

D. Essay Questions

What did Jesus mean when he said to his mother, "Did you not know that I must be in My Father's house?"

_____

_____

_____

Joseph and Mary worried about Jesus because they loved him. How do your parents show their love for you?

_____

_____

_____

The Story of John the Baptist
Matthew 3, Mark 1:1-11, Luke 3:1-22

When Jesus was quietly preparing for His mission, God had made ready another great voice in the work of redemption. **John the Baptist**, as he was later called, was a good and upright man and the son of Zacharias and Elizabeth. The prophets had **foretold** his birth as the forerunner of the Messiah. His mission was to prepare the way for Jesus' work of salvation.

John the Baptist did not bring his message to the synagogues or try to reach the people in the big cities. Instead, he preached in the thinly popu-

lated districts along the banks of the Jordan River and in the **wilderness** west of the Dead Sea. He ate only **locusts** and wild honey for food and wore a rough garment made of woven camel's hair. The theme of John's teaching was "the kingdom of heaven is at hand." He preached a message of repentance and spiritual reform. He warned every-

one who would listen that the time had come to "make straight [their] paths" and to **reform** their lives by being humble before God and truly sorry for their sins.

Things were not going well in Judea. The Jewish nation had completely lost its independence. Palestine was divided into three Roman provinces ruled by idle and greedy politicians. Even the mighty Roman Empire was weakened by the corrupt rule of Tiberius Caesar.

The state of religion in Judea had fallen so low that the sacred office of the High Priest was claimed by people like Annas, and his son-in-law Caiaphas. Both of them were undeserving of respect. The religious leadership of the nation was in the hands of the rival groups of the Pharisees and the Sadducees.

Rather than leading true lives of faith these religious leaders spent most of their time **quibbling** (fighting among themselves) over the meaning of the Scriptures. Many Jewish people welcomed John's powerful message and the blessing of God through baptism by him. In fact, some of them thought that John himself was the promised Messiah. But John declared, "I am baptizing you with water, for **repentance**, but the one who is coming after me is mightier than I." He went even further saying, "I am not worthy to carry His sandals. He will **baptize** you with the Holy Spirit and fire."

John baptized thousands of people that openly **confessed** their sins and expressed a desire to turn back to God. His ministry touched the hearts of the sincere people who longed to break free of the meaningless rites and traditions made up by the corrupt Jewish priests and leaders. In fact when he saw the Pharisees and Sadducees also coming to be baptized, John dismissed them as a "**brood of vipers**."

The Jordan River where Jesus was baptized

One day after all the people had come for baptism, Jesus appeared before John and asked that He, too, should be baptized. John knew that there could be no need of repentance because he recognized who Jesus was. John protested by saying, "I need to be baptized by You and yet You are coming to me." Jesus said, "Allow it now, for thus it is fitting for us to fulfill all righteousness."

Although John did not fully understand what Jesus meant, he knew that it was important for him to baptize Jesus. Then, as Jesus came up out of the water, the heavens were suddenly opened and, the Spirit of God descended upon Jesus in the form of a **dove**. Then the voice of God was heard to say, "This is My beloved Son, with whom I am well pleased."

The voice of God had made it perfectly clear to John what he had just done. He knew then that God had used him to baptize the long promised Messiah, the **Lamb of God**, who was sent as the Savior of the world.

Name: _____ Date: _____

Key Words - The Story of John the Baptist

baptize	dove	Lamb of God	reform
brood of vipers	foretold	locusts	repentance
confessed	John the Baptist	quibbling	wilderness

A. Two different Baptisms

Use the answer bank below to complete the following sentences. Use the letters in front of each correct answer to reveal the corresponding numbered blank in statement #11. Use the letters behind each correct answer to reveal the corresponding numbered blank in statement #12.

Answer bank

S = baptize = N   Y = reform = E

L = locusts = P   R = quibbling = N

I = dove = A   T = wilderness = E

P = brood of vipers = T   I = confessed = C

H = foretold = R   O = John the Baptist = E

1. The prophets _____ Jesus' birth.

2. _____ _____ _____ prepared the way for Jesus.

3. John ate _____ and honey while in the wilderness.

4. John the Baptist told people to change or _____ their lives.

5. John would _____ people with the water of the Jordan River.

6. John called the Pharisees and Sadducees a _____ ____ _____.

7. The Spirit of God descended upon Jesus in the form of a _____.

8. The Pharisees and Sadducees were arguing or _____.

9. John baptized the people who _____ their sins.

10. John the Baptist lived in the _____.

Mystery words:

11. Jesus was baptized with __ __ __ __ __ __ __ __ __ __.
    1 2 3 4   5 6 7 8 9 10

12. John the Baptist called for __ __ __ __ __ __ __ __ __ __.
    1 2 3 4 5 6 7 8 9 10

B. Word Search

Find and circle the 12 **key word(s)** in the word search puzzle below.

```
B C O N F E S S E D C H U J
T R H N F O R E T O L D O R
H E O L J E S U S W O H R M
E P L O W I L D E R N E S S
T E Y C D E E H R T D S K E
D N S U F O R E H N L T T Z
I T P S F E F E E D O V E I
E A I T R O B V H T T O W T
E N R S R A B E I E E N B P
N C I M P R A B N P R A R A
D E T T O V E F E S E S E B
Q U I B B L I N G O F R E R
R S M J O H N W I L D E S R
T H E B I D O G F O B M A L
```

baptize

brood of vipers

confessed

dove

foretold

John the Baptist

Lamb of God

locusts

quibbling

reform

repentance

wilderness

C. Essay Questions

What was John the Baptist trying to get the people to do? Why was this important?

_____

_____

_____

Is there a need for reform and repentance today? Explain.

_____

_____

_____

The Story of the Twelve Apostles
Matt 10: 1-15; Mark 3: 13-18

As His ministry grew, word about Jesus spread very quickly. He was followed by great multitudes from all parts of Galilee and from Judea. People even came from Idumea and from the land beyond the Jordan River. People came from as far away as the Phenician cities of Tyre and Sidon. There were so many people at times that Jesus could not even walk through the crowds without being mobbed. Great throngs of people with all kinds of ailments pressed forward to see and hear Him. Jesus healed hundreds of these people through loving words or a touch.

But Jesus knew that these demands on Him were growing too large. He could not **minister** to each and every one of those who came to see, hear and touch Him. In order to speak to the crowds, Jesus would often get into a boat and shove it away from the shore so everyone could see Him. More and more people came each day. Finally, Jesus said to His **disciples**, "The harvest is abundant but the laborers are few."

Jesus also knew that He would not be among His followers much longer. He summoned some of the disciples to the mountain where He had gone to pray. He appointed these twelve men to be His **Apostles**. Apostle means "one who is sent."

Each of these Apostles had lived with Jesus and shared His daily life. They all witnessed His teaching and miracles as well as His struggles with the Scribes and **Pharisees**. They each were sent out into Israel and other distant lands to pro-

claim the good news that Jesus was the **Messiah** the Israelites were waiting for. They were each given the power to heal the sick and to cast out demons as proof of the truth of their testimony.

The Apostles were handpicked by God through Jesus. They were just ordinary people. None were educated Rabbis or prominent Jewish community leaders. However, they were given unusual intellectual ability. This is evident in the writings of some members of the group, and in their wonderful deeds in promoting the kingdom of Jesus after His **Ascension** into heaven. Four of them, Matthew, Mark, Luke and John are among the foremost writers of the New Testament.

By virtue of his powers of leadership and vigorous character, Peter became the spokesman of the Apostles. The superior force of his character revealed itself in the vigor of his writings and deeds. Along with his faith, Jesus recognized these qualities in him and named him the rock on which [He] would build [His] church." For this reason, we recognize Peter as the first **Pope** of the church.

John's writings, as well as the recorded events of his life, show that he was a profound, imaginative thinker. Matthew's history of the teachings and deeds of Jesus displays the grasp of a real scholar in his knowledge of Old Testament **prophecies**. James must have been outstanding in his ability to present the gospel of Jesus, for he was the first of the noble company to suffer martyrdom. Judas Iscariot was the "wolf in sheep's clothing." He showed his selfish, greedy nature on several occasions, and finally betrayed Jesus into the hands of His enemies in the **Garden of Gethsemane**.

Little is known of the other Apostles beyond the fact that they remained loyal to Jesus. They proclaimed God's message with Him while Jesus was alive. Then, they spread the gospel throughout the world after His Ascension. The Apostles were **witnesses** to the fact that Jesus rose from the dead. God **anointed** them with the Holy Spirit on **Pentecost**. Most of them died martyrs as testimony to their faith in God and His son Jesus Christ.

Key Words - The Story of the Twelve Apostles

anointed	disciples	minister	Pope
Apostles	Garden of Gethsemane	Pentecost	prophecies
Ascension	Messiah	Pharisees	witnesses

A. Find-a-Word Quiz

The **key words** below are missing two or more letters. The missing parts of the key words are hidden in the letter box. Find and cross out the missing letters as you use them. Then, place them in the spaces to complete the **key words**. Unscramble the remaining letters to reveal the mystery words.

a__ __ __ __les

__ __ __ __iples

__ __ __ __ster

as__ __ __sion

Mess__ __ __

Pro__ __ __ __ies

__ __pe

Pha__ __ __ __ __s

Witne__ __ __ __

__ __ __inted

Pente__ __ __ __

Garden of __ __ __ __semane

```
p  g  a  n  e  c  h
a  u  e  i  s  o  n
i  o  e  s  e  s  c
a  t  d  t  e  t  h
s  s  j  d  g  L  a
s  o  L  m  i  n  i
e  p  o  e  s  i  e
p  e  h  c  c  r  i
```

Mystery Words:

_____ & _____
(these are not key words)

B. True or False

Put a T in front of the statements that are true. Put an F in front of the statements that are false.

_____1. Jesus chose Apostles since he was having difficulty ministering to all the people by Himself.

_____2. The Pharisees were very helpful to Jesus.

_____3. James betrayed Jesus in the Garden of Gesthemane.

_____4. The Apostles were witnesses that Jesus rose from the dead.

_____5. Peter is recognized as the first Pope of the Catholic church.

_____6. The Apostles promoted the kingdom of Christ after Jesus' Ascension.

C. Matching

Match the **key word(s)** on the left with the correct word or phrase on the right.

_____ Apostles

_____ Disciples

_____ Minister

_____ Ascension

_____ Messiah

_____ Prophecies

_____ Pope

_____ Pharisees

_____ Witnesses

_____ Garden of Gesthemene

_____ Pentecost

A. rising up

B. where Jesus prayed

C. the leader of the Catholic church

D. one who is sent

E. they saw Jesus after His resurrection

F. the followers of Christ

G. to teach and/or give aid

H. Jesus

I. predictions

J. a group of Jewish leaders

K. the apostles were anointed this day

D. Essay Questions

Name some of the things all the Apostles had in common?

_____

_____

_____

_____

The Apostles gave Jesus help to spread the Gospel. How do you help spread Jesus' message?

_____

_____

_____

_____

The Story of the Wedding at Cana

John 2: 1-11

One day, shortly after beginning His public ministry, Jesus was in Cana to attend a wedding celebration. **Cana** was a small town in Galilee not too far from Jesus' boyhood home of Nazareth. A wonderful event took place. During this feast, Jesus performed His first **miracle** to demonstrate to His disciples and those who saw Him that He truly was the Son of God.

In some ways, weddings in Jesus' time were a lot like they are today. Families and friends traveled from near and far to gather and celebrate with the new bride and groom. These occasions were very happy with plenty of time planned for visiting and enjoying family and friends. In other ways, these **celebrations** were much different than the ones we attend today. At that time, it was often very difficult to travel from place to place. Without the conveniences of cars or airplanes that we enjoy today, people often had to use the simplest forms of transportation possible. Most of them probably walked so it took days or maybe weeks to get from place to place.

Therefore, it was normal for weddings and other family celebrations in Jesus' day to last for several days, even as long as a week. Many members of **Jewish** families probably didn't get to see each other except at these very special occasions. Therefore, this **tradition** of celebrating longer was probably a very good thing for everyone involved. Mary and Joseph might have been close friends

of the wedding couple or their parents at Cana. That is why Jesus and His followers would also have been invited. We don't know exactly when Jesus arrived but

it may have been two or three days after the wedding celebration began. Soon after Jesus arrived, it came to Mary's attention that the supply of **wine** was about to run out. Mary knew what an **embarrassment** this would be to the hosts so she quickly reported the problem to her son saying; "They have no wine." Jesus had never attempted to use the wonderful powers God had given Him but Mary sensed that the time had come for Him to prove His Divinity by performing a miracle.

In reply to His mother's appeal Jesus said, "Woman, how does your concern affect me? My hour has not yet come." Even though Mary may not have understood exactly what Jesus meant by this, she immediately went to the servers and said, "**Do whatever He tells you**."

Out of respect for His mother and for the help she was trying to provide, Jesus responded to the wedding family's need. Now there were six stone water jars setting there for Jewish ceremonial washings. Each could hold twenty to **thirty gallons**. Jesus told the servants to "Fill the jars with water." So, they filled each of the jars with water - bringing to Him as much as **180 gallons**. Then He told them, "Draw some out now and take it to the **headwaiter**." So they took it. When the headwaiter had tasted the water that was now turned into wine, he was amazed. He called the bridegroom and said to

him "Everyone serves the good wine first, and then when people have drunk freely, an inferior one; but you have kept the good wine until now." Only the servants that had filled the **stone water jars**, His disciples and those sitting close to Jesus, knew what had really happened. The other guests at the feast probably did not know a miracle had taken place. They simply were amazed at the quality of the wine.

At Cana, Jesus showed His love for all humanity by thinking of the well-being of others before Himself. His miracle demonstrated His love for all the guests - no matter what their social status and proved to His disciples that He was the "anointed one" sent from His Father in heaven.

Name: _____ Date: _____

Key Words - The Story of the Wedding at Cana

180 gallons	embarrassment	stone water jars
Cana	headwaiter	thirty gallons
celebrations	Jewish	tradition
Do whatever He tells you	miracle	wine

A. Scrambled Letters

The paired or single letters in the water jars form the key word(s) to answer the clues below. To determine the answers, choose a letter or group of letters from the first jar to begin each word. The letters or groups of letters from the second jar form the middle of each word. The letters or groups of letters from the third jar form the end of each word. Hint: The number of letters in each word are at the end of the line before the clue. When you have finished the clues, the remaining pairs of letters will reveal the mystery answer below.

1. _____ (7) Jesus performed this at Cana.

2. _____ (6) Jesus' family was

3. _____ (4) a drink made from grapes

4. _____ (10) the person that served the wine

5. _____ (4) the town where the wedding occurred

Mystery Answer _____ (5)

B. Word Search

Find and circle 10 of the 12 **key words**.

```
D O W H A T E V E R H E T E L L S Y O U
I L L O M H I R T S S A N R R D T A W Y
T O Y S V I C H A I R R E C N U O O B O
I T N T A R R M E R I F M N J A N C K Y
O R N R E T Y A P U M P S K I E E T E O
N A B A E Y S U C O M Y S E K C W I M U
T B L D A G N K E L T D A I C I A I T Z
S N O I T A R B E L E C R N N O T I S W
G T V T K L O O B Y R A R E L A E N D H
E E I I K O O C C D R I A B A G R I B A
R M O O N O S T E R J O B H N N J M A T
R E B N A N Z I L E S I M R O D A K R I
P I G L E S T F L A S H E L I G R C H O
J E S U R E T I A W D A E H P O S O H N
```

180 gallons   embarrassment   stone water jars
Cana   headwaiter   thirty gallons
celebrations   Jewish   tradition
Do whatever He tells you   miracle   wine

C. Essay Questions

Why do you think it was important for Jesus to perform miracles?

_____

_____

_____

How and when are both water and wine important in the practice of your faith?

_____

_____

_____

The Story of the Sermon on the Mount
Matt 5:1-7:27

One day, several thousand people had gathered around Jesus and His disciples. He went up on the side of a mountain so that He could be seen and heard by all. The talk He gave that day is known as the **Sermon on the Mount**. In it, Jesus taught all those **assembled** how to live each day in a manner pleasing to God. He explained that God judges our thoughts as well as what we say and do.

Jesus' simple message was not what many Jewish people expected to hear. Most of them had been taught that the Messiah God had promised would bring back the wealth and worldwide power of the Israelite empire of long ago. That is why most of them misunderstood who Jesus actually was. Jesus' message that day revealed to the crowd that His kingdom was not of this world but instead a spiritual kingdom. He assured them that His kingdom was one that would flourish in spite of opposition and persecution.

Jesus also shared The **Beatitudes** as guidelines on the way to live. They describe the kind of people in His kingdom this way: **Blessed** are . .

1) the poor in spirit - not too proud to ask God's help or too self-satisfied;

2) they who mourn - feeling the sadness and loss that is caused by sin;

3) the **meek** - not stubborn or quick tempered, but gentle and forgiving;

4) they who hunger and thirst for righteousness - striving to obey God;

5) the merciful - sympathetic, helpful and generous;

6) the clean of heart - doing right in both thoughts and intentions;

7) the peacemakers - seeking peace in a world torn by strife and hatred;

8) the **persecuted** - mistreated for God's sake for doing the right thing.

Jesus also taught **The Lord's Prayer** as an example of a way to pray. His simplest lesson that day was what we know as **The Golden Rule**. It's words are simple, "Do to others whatever you would have them do to you." Jesus explained to the people that they should love their enemies and "pray for those who persecute you."

He cautioned the people that **worship** and prayer should not be done just for others to see. Instead, it should be private time with God. **Giving** also was to be done in secret so that your "left hand [does not] know what your right hand is doing."

Dependance on money and material possessions was another warning Jesus gave the people. He told them not to spend all their time worrying about their daily needs of

Knock and the door will be opened to you.

food, shelter and clothing. He instructed them to "Seek first the kingdom [of God] and His righteousness." Jesus assured them God our Heavenly Father loves and cares for us as His children. He told the people: "Ask and it will be given to you; seek and you will find; knock and the door will be opened to you. For everyone who asks, receives; and the one who seeks, finds; and to the one who knocks, the door will be opened."

"Stop **judging**, that you may not be judged. For as you judge, so will you be judged.." was another lesson Jesus taught that day. He told the people that cleaning up the sins in their own lives would keep them so busy that they wouldn't have time to worry about the sins of others.

Jesus realized that living according to God's rules was not going to be easy for us. Not everyone is able to do it all the time. However, He assured us that "everyone who listens to these words of Mine and acts on them will be like a **wise man** who built his house on rock. ." which is stable and strong instead of on sand which washes away.

Name: _____ Date: _____

Key Words - The Story of the Sermon on the Mount

assembled	judging	Sermon on the Mount	The Lord's Prayer
blessed	meek	Beatitudes	wise man
giving	persecuted	The Golden Rule	worship

A. Mount of Consonants

The **key words** are missing their consonants. Each letter is used only once.

1. ___ i ___ e ___ a ___

2. ___ i ___ i ___ ___

3. ___ o ___ ___ ___ i ___

4. ___ u ___ ___ i ___ ___

5. ___ e e ___

6. ___ e a ___ i ___ u ___ e ___

7. ___ ___ e ___ ___ e ___

8. a ___ ___ e ___ ___ ___ e ___

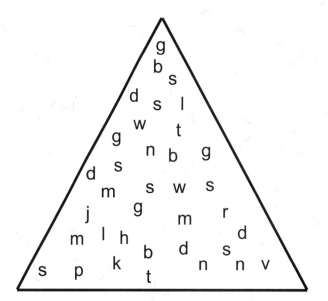

B. Matching

Match the **key word(s)** on the left with the correct word or phrase on the right.

_____Sermon on the Mount   A. eight guidelines for a way to live

_____The Beatitudes   B. evaluating someone else

_____The Lord's Prayer   C. a lesson of how to treat others

_____The Golden Rule   D. not stubborn, gentle

_____Assembled   E. Jesus'mountainside talk

_____Blessed   F. a benefit of living The Beatitudes

_____Persecuted   G. Jesus gave us this prayer

_____Meek   H. gathered together

_____Judging   I. mistreated for God's sake

_____Worship   J. he builds his house on the a rock

_____Giving   K. donating, volunteering

_____Wise man   L. praise

C. Fill in the Blanks

Fill in the blanks with the correct word(s) to complete the Beatitudes. Then, put them in the correct order below.

A. the _____, not stubborn but gentle

B. the _____, helpful and generous

C. the _____, good in thought and intentions

D. the _____, suffer for God's sake

E. the _____, settles arguments and fights

F. the _____, not too proud to ask God's help

G. they who _____, try to obey God

H. they who_____, feel sadness

Correct order ___ ___ ___ ___ ___ ___ ___ ___
               1   2   3   4   5   6   7   8

D. Essay Questions

Did Jesus think that we could <u>always</u> do as He expected? When we don't do what He expects of us, what Sacrament is available to help us? Explain.

_____

_____

_____

How are the The Beatitudes like the Ten Commandments?

_____

_____

_____

The Story of the Raising of Lazarus
John 11:1-53

While Jesus was traveling and teaching in the villages surrounding Judea, there was a crisis in Bethany. His dear friend **Lazarus** became very sick. **Mary** and **Martha**, his sisters, sent a message to Jesus to tell Him of their brother's illness. Being true believers of Jesus, they were sure that their brother would not die if He were there. These were people Jesus had visited whenever He was in their area. He and His disciples enjoyed eating and relaxing with these faithful and loving friends.

Before the message reached Jesus, Lazarus had already died. Two days passed before Jesus began his journey to Bethany. On deciding to return, Jesus said to his disciples, "Our friend Lazarus is asleep, but I am going to awaken him." The disciples did not understand that Jesus knew that Lazarus had already died. They were puzzled why Jesus said he was asleep. So Jesus said to them very clearly, "Lazarus has died. And I am glad for you that I was not there, that you may believe."

Two more days passed before Jesus and the disciples reached Bethany. When they arrived, they learned that Lazarus had been in the **tomb** for four days. Martha went out to meet Jesus, saying, "Lord, if You had been here, my brother would not have died." Even though her brother had been buried for four days, she proved her **faith** in Jesus by saying, "I know that whatever You ask of God, God will give You." When Jesus replied, "Your brother will rise," Martha thought that He was talking about the final **resurrection** on the last day. She believed as Jesus had taught that all those who have died would be raised from the dead on the last day. Sadly, she thought that Lazarus would not rise again until then. Then Jesus said the most beautiful words to further explain. "I am the resurrection and the life; whoever believes in Me, even if he dies, will live, and everyone who lives and believes in Me will never die." Jesus asked Martha if she believed Him. She said, "Yes, Lord, I have come to believe that You are the **Messiah**, the Son of God, the one who is coming into the world." What Jesus said that day is so important to us. Because of His words, we know that when a member of our family or a friend, or anyone who believes in Jesus dies, they truly never really die but will one day live with Him in heaven forever.

What Jesus said so strengthened the faith of Martha that she hurried to bring her sister the good news that Jesus had come. Mary, followed by many of the Jews that had come to comfort her and her sister, rushed out to meet Jesus. Like Martha, Mary expressed her faith in Jesus. Jesus asked Mary, "Where have you laid him?" Jesus loved Lazarus so much that even He **wept** on his way to the tomb! Some of the Jews who opposed Him said, "Could not the one, who opened the eyes of the blind man have done something so that this man would not have died?"

When Jesus arrived at the place where Lazarus was buried, Jesus commanded His disciples to roll away the stone. After a prayer of thanksgiving to God, Jesus cried out in a loud voice, "Lazarus, come out!" Immediately, Lazarus walked out of the tomb with all the **burial garments** (that were a tradition then) still wrapped around him. Jesus then told his disciples, "Untie him and let him go."

The **miracle** of raising Lazarus from the dead led many Jewish people to accept Jesus as the Messiah. However, it convinced the chief priests and other leaders of both the Pharisees and Sadducees to further mistrust Him. The **Sanhedrin** (the Jewish court) – composed of scribes and chief priests decided that they had to get rid of Jesus permanently. **Caiaphas**, the acting High Priest, led the plot to kill Jesus out of jealousy and in order to avoid trouble with the Roman authorities.

Key Words - The Story of the Raising of Lazarus

burial garments	Lazarus	Messiah	Sanhedrin
Caiaphas	Martha	miracle	tomb
faith	Mary	resurrection	wept

A. Magic Square

Match the **key word(s)** on the left with the correct phrase on the right. Then place the number from column #1 in the correct box in the "magic square." You will have all the answers correct if each column going across, down and diagonally adds up to 34.

A	B	C	D
E	16	13	F
15	G	H	14
I	J	K	L

Column #1

1. Messiah
2. Tomb
3. Resurrection
4. Wept
5. Mary
6. Miracle
7. Sanhedrin
8. Caiaphas
9. Lazarus
10. Martha
11. Burial garments
12. Faith

Column #2

_____A. Lazarus' sister that went to meet Jesus

_____B. Martha's sister

_____C. the acting High Priest

_____D. Lazarus wore these

_____E. the raising from the dead

_____F. where Lazarus was when Jesus arrived

_____G. Jesus did this on the way to the tomb

_____H. the Son of God

_____I. a supernatural act of God

_____J. Jesus' friend who died from illness

_____K. Martha proved her _____ in Jesus

_____L. the Jewish court

B. True or False

Circle the letter in the first column for each statement that is true. Circle the letter in the second column for each statement that is false. Then place letters in the blanks at bottom to reveal the mystery verse.

T	F	
J	H	1. Mary and Martha were Lazarus' sisters.
O	E	2. Jesus had never met Lazarus before.
I	S	3. Jesus arrived at Lazarus' house just as he was dying.
U	S	4. Martha proved her faith in Jesus by saying "I know that whatever You ask God, God will give You."
S	A	5. Martha believed that Jesus was the Messiah.
W	A	6. As Jesus walked to Lazarus' tomb, He wept.
I	E	7. Lazarus' sisters were putting burial garments on him when Jesus raised him from the dead.
P	V	8. Many Jews accepted Jesus as the Messiah after this miracle.
E	T	9. The Sanhedrin believed in Jesus after learning of this miracle

John 11:35 ___ ___ ___ ___ ___   ___ ___ ___ ___.
           1   2   3   4   5   6   7   8   9

C. Essay Questions

What did Jesus mean when He said, "I am the resurrection and the life?"

_____

_____

_____

Jesus showed His love for His friend Lazarus when He wept for him after he died. Have you ever felt the need to cry, like Jesus did, after learning of the sickness or death of a family member or a friend? Explain.

_____

_____

_____

The Story of the Last Supper
Matthew 26, Mark 14, Luke 22, John 13

One of the most important events in the life of every Jewish family is the celebration of the Feast of Passover. For seven days each Spring the Jewish people remember the time when their ancestors were freed from slavery in Egypt and led by Moses to the Promised Land. A traditional part of this celebration has always been the sharing of the **Passover Meal**.

The Passover meal of lamb, bitter herbs and unleavened bread is very symbolic. In fact, Jewish law prescribed every part of this meal and how to celebrate it. For instance, the lamb is served to recall the blood that was shed that marked the doorposts to save the Israelites from the final plague on Egypt. The bitter **herbs** are served to remind all of the bitter time of **slavery** in Egypt.

The unleavened bread is served as a reminder of how quickly the Jewish people responded to God during the **exodus** from Egypt.

Knowing that He was soon to die, Jesus' plan was to gather the disciples in Jerusalem so they could celebrate the Passover meal (the meal we call the **Last Supper**). On the first day of the Feast of the Unleavened Bread as it was also called, Jesus sent Peter and John into Jerusalem to make these preparations for them. He told them that they would meet a certain man carrying a jar of water. They were to follow him and say to his master, "The teacher says, 'My appointed time draws near; in your house I shall celebrate the Passover with My disciples.'" Jesus told them that he would show them an **upper room** furnished and ready. They found everything exactly as Jesus had said.

When it was time to eat, Jesus and the other disciples arrived and sat at the table. The disciples all watched in disbelief as Jesus, the Master, rose from the table, shed His robe and tied a towel around His waist. Then He took a jar of water and a basin; one by one He washed the **feet** of the Apostles. All of them sat in humble silence except Peter who said to Him, "You will never wash my feet." Then Jesus told Peter that if he belonged to Him, he must allow Jesus to wash his feet. Then Peter agreed. Finishing up, Jesus told His disciples that He had just given them an example to follow. Jesus taught us with His humble actions that, no matter who we are, it is only in **serving** others that we truly serve God.

Later, Jesus also said that one of them was going to betray Him and that it would be better for him if he had not been born. Knowing Jesus was talking about him, Judas got up and left. He had made a deal with the chief priests and scribes to **betray** Jesus for 30 pieces of silver.

Jesus then told the rest of the disciples many things that were going to happen. He said He was going to die soon. They were all very sad. Then He took the **bread**, blessed it, and broke it and gave it to them saying, "Take and eat; this is My body." Likewise, He took a cup of **wine**, blessed it and gave it to them saying, "Drink from it, all of you, for this is My blood of the covenant, which will be shed for the forgiveness of sin. Do this in memory of Me."

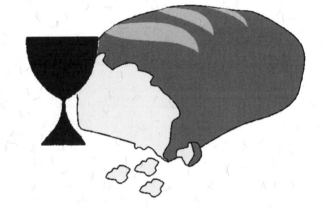

This was Jesus' greatest gift. When we participate in the Celebration of the **Eucharist,** we witness again this beautiful gift Jesus gave His church. God blesses us through the gift of His son in Holy Communion as real to us today as it was to His disciples the night of the Last Supper.

Jesus concluded the Last Supper by telling His disciples; "I am the way and the truth and the life. No one comes to the Father except through Me. If you know Me, then you will also know My Father." He commanded them to, "As I have loved you, so you also should love one another. This is how all will know that you are My disciples, if you have love for one another."

When they finished the meal, Jesus and the disciples probably sang the traditional Passover songs. Then, Jesus left to go to the Mount of Olives to pray. Some of the disciples followed Him.

Name: _____ Date: _____

Key Words - The Story of the Last Supper

betray	Eucharist	Passover Meal	upper room
herbs	Exodus	serving	feet
bread	Last Supper	slavery	wine

A. Crossword

Fill in the squares with the **key word(s)** to complete the statements below.

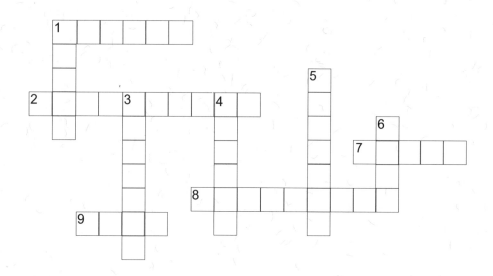

Across

1. Judas was to _____ Jesus for 30 pieces of silver.
2. Jesus ate the _____ with His disciples in the upper room.
7. At the Passover meal bitter _____ were served to remind the Israelites of their days of slavery in Egypt.
8. The Celebration of the _____
9. The cup of _____ became Jesus' blood shed for the forgiveness of our sins.

Down

1. The _____ became the body of Jesus.
3. Jesus taught us by His example that we should be _____ others.
4. During the _____ from Egypt the Israelites ate unleavened bread.
5. The Israelites were freed from _____ in Egypt.
6. Jesus washed the _____ of the Apostles to teach how to serve others.

B. Missing Words

Fill in the blanks to spell the **key word(s)**. Then transfer the numbered letters into the blanks to reveal the answer to the mystery question.

1. Bitter h__ __ __ __ were served at the Passover meal.

            4

2. The Israelites left __ __ __ __ __ __y in Egpyt to go to the Promised Land.

           12   8

3. Jesus shared the Passover meal in the __ __ __ __ r r __ __ __.

          1   9

4. Jesus w __ __ __ __ __ the __ __ __t of all the disciples before they ate.

        11   10

5. Jesus taught us that by __ __ __ __ __ __ g others we are truly serving God.

              6

6. In the __ __ l __ __ __ __ t __ __ __ of the E __ __ __ __ __ __ __ __ we see

        7   5   2   3

    Jesus' gift to His believers.

Mystery question: What special meal were Jesus and the disciples sharing?

___ ___ ___ ___ ___ ___ ___ ___   ___ ___ ___ ___
 1   2   3   4   5   6   7   8   9 10 11 12

C. Essay Questions

Why did Jesus wash the Apostles' feet?

_____

_____

_____

_____

What opportunities do you have to serve others?

_____

_____

_____

_____

The Story of the Crucifixion and Resurrection of Jesus
Matt. 26-28, Mk. 14-16, Lk. 22-24, Jn. 18-20

After the Last Supper, Jesus led the disciples to the **Garden of Gethsemane** where He frequently went to pray. Going off a little distance from the group, He prayed so intensely to God about the up-coming events that He sweat large drops of blood. Several times He went back to check on the disciples who were sup-posed to be praying and watching but each time they were sleeping. Finally, He awakened them to tell them that He was about to be **betrayed**. Just then soldiers and a mob arrived. **Judas** came forward greeting Jesus with a kiss as a signal that this was the man to arrest. Without think-ing, Peter drew his sword and cut off one man's ear. Jesus gently scolded Peter saying, "Don't you know that My Father would send 10,000 angels to protect Me if I asked. But I came to fulfill the scriptures and God's promises." He told the soldiers to let the others go so the disciples and many of those who were following Jesus ran away.

Binding Him, the temple guards led Jesus off to one of several trials that filled the night. He was questioned before Annas, the father-in-law of Caiaphas the High Priest. Then Annas sent Him to Caiaphas. The Sanhedrin that had gathered there accused and judged Jesus on the basis of lies from false witnesses. Then the soldiers hit Him, spit on Him and mocked Him.

Peter, who had followed them at a safe distance, joined the servants around a fire in Caiaphas' courtyard, but he was recognized as a disciple. Just as the Lord had said, Peter **denied** ever knowing Jesus three times before the rooster crowed. When he realized what he had done, Peter ran away weeping.

Shortly after dawn Jesus was sent to the palace of **Pontius Pilate** the

Roman governor. Pilate questioned Him asking "Are you king of the Jews?" Jesus answered "You say so." Then He stood quietly while the Jewish leaders continued to accuse Him. When Pilate learned Jesus was from Nazareth he sent Him to **Herod** because Galilee was under his jurisdiction.

Herod was delighted to have Jesus brought before him because he hoped to see Him perform a miracle. Once again, Jesus remained silent. So Herod allowed his soldiers to put a robe and crown of thorns on Him while they abused Him before sending Him back to Pilate.

Again Pilate tried to reason with the Sanhedrin telling them neither he nor Herod could find any fault with Jesus. He said that he would have Jesus scourged and release Him, but they demanded that He be **crucified**. Even though Pilate yielded to the will of the crowd sentencing Jesus to death, he ceremoniously washed his hands in front of the crowd saying, "I am innocent of this man's blood ."

After beating Jesus, the soldiers laid the cross on His bloody back and shoulders and led Him away. The Lord was so weak that He fell several times under the weight of the cross. Simon of Cyrene was in the crowd lining the street and was forced to carry the cross for Jesus. When they arrived at **Golgotha** meaning "the Skull," soldiers nailed Jesus to the cross then placed a sign over His head that read, "This is the King of the Jews." As He hung up there with criminals on either side of Him, the soldiers **cast lots** (gambled) for His clothes - His only earthly possessions. Meanwhile, the Jewish leaders jeered at Him, "If you are king of the Jews, save yourself!"

Even while suffering such physical and mental distress, Jesus prayed, "Father, forgive them, they know not what they do." Finally, when He had breathed His last breath a soldier thrust a sword into His side. Faithful believers quickly took down His body, bound it with burial cloths and put in a new tomb belonging to Joseph of Arimathea because the **Jewish Sabbath** began at sundown.

But the good news is that Jesus didn't stay in the tomb! On the **third day** when the women went to properly prepare the body according to Jewish custom, they found only an empty cave and the burial cloths! Suddenly, two angels appeared announcing Jesus' resurrection from the dead! Jesus was God's greatest gift to mankind. On the cross, He became the sacrificial lamb for the **atonement** (forgiveness) for our sins. In His resurrection, Jesus triumphed over sin and death and gives us hope for eternal life with Him.

Key Words - The Story of the Crucifixion and Resurrection of Jesus

atonement	crucified	Golgatha	Judas
betrayed	denied	Herod	Pontius Pilate
cast lots	Garden of Gethsemane	Jewish Sabbath	third day

A. Crossword Puzzle

Fill in the squares with the **key word(s)** to complete the statements below.

Down

1. where Jesus often went to pray
2. Galilee was his jurisdiction
4. the soldiers did this for Jesus' clothes
5. sundown was the beginning of this
8. on this day women went to the tomb

Across

3. Jesus sentence was to be...
6. Peter _____ ever knowing Jesus
7. the Roman governor at the time
9. the place called "the skull"
10. He greeted Jesus with a kiss
11. Jesus was __ for 30 pieces of silver
12. forgiveness

B. True or False Mystery Word

Circle the letter in the first column before each statement that is true. Circle the letter in the second column before each statement that is false. The circled letters spell the mystery word.

T	**F**	
F	R	1. The disciples prayed with Jesus in Garden of Gesthemane.
E	K	2. Jesus sweat blood because He prayed so intensely.
R	S	3. Judas drew his sword and struck a soldier when they tried to take Jesus captive.
U	L	4. Jesus said He came to fulfill scriptures and obey God.
R	O	5. Pontius Pilate sent Jesus to Herod
R	Z	6. Herod hoped to see Jesus perform a miracle.
G	E	7. Herod yielded to the crowd by sentencing Jesus to be crucified.
C	P	8. Pilate washed his hands and said he was innocent of taking Jesus' life.
W	T	9. The soldiers made Peter carry Jesus' cross.
I	D	10. Jesus hung on the cross with criminals on either side of Him.
O	H	11. Believers put Jesus' body into a new tomb.
N	U	12. On third day women went to tomb to prepare Jesus' body.

Mystery word ___ ___ ___ ___ ___ ___ ___ ___ ___ ___ ___ ___

C. Essay Questions

Why did Jesus get upset with Peter for cutting off the servant's ear?

_____

_____

_____

Peter denied knowing Jesus to stay out of trouble. Have you ever been afraid or ashamed to admit that you believe in Jesus?

_____

_____

_____

The Story of the Road to Emmaus
Luke 24:13-35

Late one evening shortly after Jesus rose from the dead, two of His disciples were walking along the road. They were headed toward **Emmaus**, a village about seven miles from Jerusalem. The two **disciples** were sharing their thoughts on what had happened to Jesus during the past few days. Suddenly they were approached and joined by another man. It was Jesus, but their eyes were prevented from recognizing Him. To them, Jesus was simply a **stranger** - just another man, like them, walking along the road.

Jesus asked them, "What are you discussing?" In amazement, one of the disciples, whose name was Cleopas, said to Jesus, "Are you the only visitor to Jerusalem who does not know of the things that have taken place there in these days?" Jesus asked them, "What sort of things?"

The two disciples explained to "this stranger" in detail all of the terrible things that had happened to Jesus of Nazareth. They explained to their new traveling companion that Jesus was a mighty prophet sent from God who had performed many miracles and taught about the "Kingdom of God." They told of how the chief priests and rulers had handed Jesus over to the **Roman authorities** and how these authorities had put Him on trial and condemned Him to death. They even explained how Jesus had been **crucified** like a common criminal! One of the disciples said, "We had hoped that Jesus was the **Messiah** who would come to redeem our people Israel."

It is important to remember that the Israelites had been waiting for hundreds of years for God to send them a **Savior**. They did not realize that this Savior (who was Jesus) would come to reveal God's heavenly kingdom rather than simply a kingdom on earth. Like these two disciples, the Jewish people expected a political leader who would overthrow the Roman government and restore power to the Hebrew nation. They did not yet fully understand the message of salvation that Jesus had come, as man, to share.

As they continued walking, the disciples finished their story by telling "this stranger" that Jesus had been put to death on Friday. Because the **Jewish Sabbath** began at sundown, there had not been time to properly prepare His body before they laid it in the tomb. On the third day, several women had gone to the tomb to **anoint** His body with spices according to tradition. When the women arrived, it was empty! Then two angels had told them **"He is not here!"**

Jesus said to them, "Oh, how foolish you are! How slow of heart to believe all that the prophets spoke! Was it not necessary that the Messiah should suffer these things and enter into His glory?" Then beginning with Moses and all the prophets, Jesus interpreted for them all the scriptures that referred to Him.

As they neared Emmaus, Jesus acted like He was going on farther. The two men urged their new companion to stay with them. So He agreed to be their guest. While they were sharing their evening meal, Jesus took bread, said a blessing, and broke it. Instantly, in the breaking of the bread, the two disciples **recognized** who Jesus was. At that same moment, to their great disappointment, Jesus vanished.

They said to one another, "Were not our hearts burning [within us], while He spoke to us on the way and opened the scriptures to us?" They were so excited they couldn't wait to tell the other disciples what had happened so they hurried back to Jerusalem.

In this story, Jesus reminds us how often we fail to recognize Him in others. We also learn, like the two disciples, that His gift of the **Holy Eucharist** is the most vivid reminder of his loving presence among us.

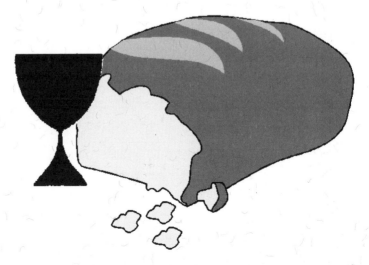

Name: _____ Date: _____

Key Words - The Story of the Road to Emmaus

anoint	Emmaus	Jewish Sabbath	Roman authorities
crucified	He is not here	Messiah	Savior
disciples	Holy Eucharist	recognized	stranger

A. Morse Code Message

Fill in the following blanks after deciphering the code represented under each letter.

A B C D E F G H I J K L M
•— —••• —•—• —•• • ••—• ——• •••• •• •——— —•— •—•• ——

N O P Q R S T U V W X Y Z
—• ——— •——• ——•— •—• ••• — ••— •••— •—— —••— —•—— ——••

1. The angels told the women at the empty tomb that ____ __ ____ ___
   •••• • •• •••

   __ _ _ __ ____ _ ___ _ .
   —• • • — •••• — •—•— —

2. Jesus of Nazareth is the ___ __ __ __ __ __ ___ and
   —— • ••• ••• •• •— ••••

   ___ __ ___ __ _ _ ___ .
   ••• •— •••— •• • • •—•—

3. Jesus was ___ __ ___ __ __ __ __ __ __ ___ .
   •• •—•— ••— ••• •• •—• •• • —••

4. Jesus was not ___ _ _ _ _ __ __ __ __ ___ by the
   •—•— • ••• • • ——• —• •• •••• — • —••

   __ __ ___ __ __ __ ___ __ __ ___ on their way to
   —•• •• ••• •• • •• ••••• —— • •••

   _ _ __ __ __ __ ___ .
   • —— —— •—• ••— •••

B. Matching

Match the **key words** on the left with the correct phrase on the right.

_____ 1. Anoint

_____ 2. Recognized

_____ 3. Stranger

_____ 4. Crucified

_____ 5. Disciples

_____ 6. Messiah

A. someone unknown

B. to be put to death

C. blessed with oil

D. Jesus' messengers to the world

E. acknowledged

F. God's chosen Redeemer

C. Essay Questions

What was Jesus doing when the two disciples he had met on the road realized who He was?

_____

_____

_____

_____

We meet people every day that don't look like they know Jesus in their hearts but after a while we learn that they do. Knowing this, how should we treat strangers that we meet everyday?

_____

_____

_____

_____

Notes

Notes